ALTERNATIVE PATHWAYS

TO THE BACCALAUREATE

ALTERNATIVE PATHWAYS TO THE BACCALAUREATE

Do Community Colleges Offer a Viable Solution to the Nation's Knowledge Deficit?

EDITED BY

Nancy Remington and Ronald Remington

Foreword by Carol D'Amico

Published in association with

Community College Baccalaureate Association

Sty/us

STERLING, VIRGINIA

Published by Stylus Publishing, LLC
22883 Quicksilver Drive
Sterling, Virginia 20166-2102

Library of Congress Cataloging-in-Publication Data
Alternative pathways to the baccalaureate : do community
colleges offer a viable solution to the nation's knowledge
deficit? / edited by Nancy Remington and Ronald Remington ;
foreword by Carol D'Amico.
     p.   cm.
   "Published in association with the Community College
Baccalaureate Association."
   Includes bibliographical references and index.
ISBN 978-1-57922-874-3 (cloth : alk. paper)
ISBN 978-1-57922-875-0 (pbk. : alk. paper)
ISBN 978-1-57922-876-7 (library networkable e-edition)
ISBN 978-1-57922-877-4 (consumer e-edition)
   1. Community colleges—United States.   2. Community
colleges—Canada.   3. Community colleges—Curricula—
United States.   4. Community colleges—Curricula—Canada.
5. Bachelor of arts degree—United States.   6. Bachelor of arts
degree—Canada.   I. Remington, Nancy, 1948–   II. Reming-
ton, Ronald, 1941–   III. Community College Baccalaureate
Association.
LB2328.A365   2013
378.1'5430973—dc23   2012013039

13-digit ISBN: 978-1-57922-874-3 (cloth)
13-digit ISBN: 978-1-57922-875-0 (paper)
13-digit ISBN: 978-1-57922-876-7 (library networkable e-edition)
13-digit ISBN: 978-1-57922-877-4 (consumer e-edition)

Printed in the United States of America

All first editions printed on acid-free paper
that meets the American National Standards Institute
Z39-48 Standard.

Bulk Purchases

Quantity discounts are available for use in workshops and
for staff development.
Call 1-800-232-0223

First Edition, 2013

10   9   8   7   6   5   4   3   2   1

"We cannot open ourselves to new insight without endangering the security of our prior assumptions. We cannot propose new ideas without risking disapproval and rejection. Creative achievement is the boldest initiative of mind, an adventure that takes its hero simultaneously to the rim of knowledge and the limits of propriety. Its pleasure is not the comfort of the safe harbor, but the thrill of reaching sail."

—Robert Grudin, *The Grace of Great Things* (1990)

CONTENTS

ACKNOWLEDGMENTS

Most worthy endeavors are not the work of one, or even a few, but of many. And so it is true with this book. Such an undertaking would not have been possible without the inspiration, generosity, guidance, and support of others. To all who have contributed, we offer our appreciation.

With special gratitude we acknowledge

- The thousands of nontraditional students who, despite financial challenges and a myriad of personal responsibilities, persevere because they understand that having a higher education will enhance their options for a richer, more fulfilling life. Their dedication serves as the book's inspiration.
- The authors and their staffs for the thoughtful, articulate discussions delineating pathways to the baccalaureate so that students may achieve their dreams. These insights provide the book's purpose.
- Most importantly, Dr. Beth Hagan, executive director of the CCBA, whose vision, caring, and tenacity made this book possible. Dr. Hagan's efforts on behalf of the CCBA advance greater access and opportunity for students in higher education. This advocacy is the book's essence.

Nancy Remington
Ronald Remington

Carol D'Amico

My first reaction when approached about writing the foreword to this book was, are they sure they are not confusing me with someone else? After all, in 2001, when I was assistant secretary for the Office of Adult and Vocational Education under President George W. Bush, I declined an invitation to keynote the Community College Baccalaureate Association's annual conference. At the time the Bush administration had no declared position on the movement, which served as my official reason for the decline, but truthfully I had my own reservations about the movement and wasn't comfortable about a tacit endorsement. My concern related to my deep commitment to the community college mission of vocational education and workforce development and how those foci would be affected by a new mission of baccalaureate education. Today my thinking is evolving for many of the reasons so well presented in this book by these learned authors.

This book does an excellent job of tracing the history of the movement and where it stands today. It discusses the political context that emerges when these discussions happen in states and the educational implications that occur when institutions take on this additional mission. For all the reasons cited by the authors, the notion of community colleges granting baccalaureate degrees is becoming much more acceptable in the United States and Canada. The primary reason for the evolution of my own thinking is very compelling—our economy is changing, and the level of education required to participate successfully in the economy is escalating—quite simply the traditional associate degree is becoming insufficient preparation for the demands of the workforce. The discussion of the Applied Baccalaureate and its place in higher education today is particularly interesting to those of us who study how to align education and the demands of the workforce.

The most interesting and topical parts of the book are the examples of the multiple ways baccalaureate education is being offered by community colleges such as online approaches in Nevada, Ohio's "3 + 1," and university partnerships in Florida and Ohio. Community colleges are once again proving to be the innovators in providing higher education, by forging unconventional partnerships with universities that create a streamlined education system. These approaches tend to be competency based and student focused, which ultimately will achieve two very important imperatives: improve affordability for students and facilitate completion in a timely fashion.

This book may or may not convert those who are concerned about "mission creep" of community colleges, but it sure will give them something to think about. As I mentioned, my own thinking is evolving, and if I were asked again to keynote the CCBA conference, I would enthusiastically accept and encourage the innovative, cost-saving approaches. However, I would also take the opportunity to talk with my colleagues in the community college world about how we need to continually work on real issues as we advocate taking on a bigger role, such as poor completion rates and extraordinary length of time to degree.

Clearly we cannot continue to do business as we have always done and expect to meet the growing demand for college-educated citizens. This book provides some thoughts on how to create a new model going forward, and it deserves serious consideration.

INTRODUCTION

Nancy Remington and Ronald Remington

This book is based on two notions: (1) Having a more highly educated citizenry is a good idea, indeed even an essential one for a strong democracy; and (2) We should be exploring and honoring models promoting just that. If you disagree with either of these notions, the ideas presented in this book will probably create an uncomfortable level of cognitive dissonance, and this book is not for you. If, however, you do agree with these notions, we believe that you will find this collection an intriguing exploration of approaches to creating greater access to the baccalaureate for a greater number of people.

So, let us proceed. We live in a time marked by exploding information technologies, a globalized economy dependent on innovation and knowledge, spiraling costs together with shrinking resources, and shifting demographics. These conditions demand more deeply educated citizens; we need people who can identify, comprehend, and then solve complex problems. Just to keep pace, education must be adept at serving a diverse population in the midst of this vertiginous change. To excel, it must do even more. Here is what is important: Higher education must provide greater, therefore more affordable, access to the acquisition of higher-level skills and knowledge for a greater proportion of the population, in essence democratizing higher education.

Although our nation has a plethora of institutions granting the baccalaureate degree, too many obstacles to obtaining this degree still exist for too many. Tuition costs have escalated rapidly, and graduates often find themselves deeply in debt. Admission standards for our prestigious institutions keep nearly all aspiring students out. Large numbers of students are underprepared. If our challenge is to provide more access for more people, so they may, in time, make significant contributions to the economy and society as well as improve their life chances for continued education and meaningful work, the big question is, "What then must we do?" Given that nearly half of all undergraduates attending college are currently enrolled in community colleges, this seems a reasonable place to begin. We present, then, in this book, some alternate pathways to the baccalaureate for consideration. All chapters included in this book have the community college as an integral part of the discussion.

A caution: In considering the various pathways to the baccalaureate, we are apt to think in terms of status and status quo—of setting up a hierarchy with which we are comfortable and then figuring out ways to maintain that hierarchy. We are susceptible to either/or thinking—putting things into categories: We attend either a two-year or four-year college; we classify institutions as either inclusive (open admission) or exclusive; we consider a course of study either academic or applied. In short, we get stuck. In an attempt to get unstuck (to overcome categorical thinking), we invite our readers to consider the contributions not as isolated solutions, but in total as a "Think Piece." According to Gilles Paquet (2006), a think piece is a specific genre, meant to be evocative, to advocate for a position, but also to promote lively discussion with both positive and negative responses. Its purpose is to encourage readers to engage in creative conflict and conversation—exploring alternatives that might otherwise never be considered. We must acknowledge here the debt of gratitude we owe to our colleague Michael Skolnik for bringing Gilles Paquet's think piece to our attention.

To begin, we offer three questions that form the core of the following chapters and from which alternate pathways emerge.

1. Is there and should there be a distinction between the applied and academic courses of study?
2. If institutions are inclusive, does that necessarily mean their programs and degrees are less rigorous and of lesser quality?
3. How can/should community colleges do more?

The contributors for the following chapters have at least three characteristics in common: They are scholars in their own right, they have achieved prominence in their respective fields, and they are deeply committed to improving higher education.

In the first chapter, Kenneth P. Walker, the founder of the Community College Baccalaureate Association, and Edith Pendleton trace the need for an informed populace in a democratic society and then attempt to bring more education to more people. They outline the founding of the Community College Baccalaureate Association and its role in helping colleges in the United States and internationally improve access, transfer rates, and completion.

Linda M. Thor and Chris Bustamante chronicle their attempt to expand the scope of Arizona's community colleges to confer the baccalaureate in chapter 2. The effort was thwarted by the state's three universities, but ironically, students came to benefit. Because this effort increased attention on the needs of underserved students, it also brought pressure for greater access and more baccalaureate options. Today, the controversy continues.

In chapter 3, John Patrick Rice discusses democratic access to higher education across the 62,000-square-mile, rural Nevada service area of Great Basin College. He presents Great Basin College as a novel kind of college— one that offers baccalaureate programs while preserving the essence of its community college roots. The tangible outcome of combining distance education technologies with baccalaureate programs for rural Nevadans is democratic access to a higher credential.

Edith Pendleton, in chapter 4, offers the personal experiences of college students as evidence of the positive impact a college degree has on their lives and their communities. Individually, these personal accounts are powerful; collectively, they make a compelling case for the benefits of greater access to higher education.

Because the traditional missions of community colleges offering baccalaureate degrees are necessarily evolving, regional accrediting agencies face continuing challenges. In chapter 5, Belle S. Wheelan and her colleague Tom Benberg address the issues of quality and uniqueness of degrees for community colleges through the lens of regional accreditation.

Alene Bycer Russell provides a national update of the community college baccalaureate in chapter 6. Although some community colleges have been offering the degree for more than 20 years, she notes that these programs are still regarded as unique and explores the current as well as future needs.

The Division of Florida Colleges has recently surged ahead as a leader in increasing access to the baccalaureate through a groundswell of newly offered applied and workforce baccalaureate degrees. In chapter 7, Deborah L. Floyd and Angela M. Garcia Falconetti, in addition to describing the evolution of the Community College Baccalaureate movement in Florida, use student and program data to carefully document major changes in Florida's higher educational system.

In chapter 8, Collin M. Ruud and Debra D. Bragg address the novelty of "applied baccalaureate" degrees. They acknowledge the need for an avenue of transfer for applied associate degree programs and cite a national survey of applied baccalaureate degrees in the workforce, discussing potential implications for higher education.

Drawing on his vast experience with Canadian higher education, Michael L. Skolnik in chapter 9 probes the comparison of traditional academic baccalaureate degrees with the new, more workforce-oriented degrees most often offered by community colleges. Additionally, he explores the essentials surrounding the concept, nature, operationalized practice, and status of an applied degree.

Lisa Romano-Arnold and Marie Cini in chapter 10 examine online access to the baccalaureate degree. They identify several areas of concern in the 2 + 2 transfer model as community college students move on to access university upper-division courses, and they conclude with practices that successfully address these concerns.

When regulating entities will not authorize community colleges to award baccalaureate degrees, some community colleges have found benefits in partnering with universities. More than 15 years ago, the notion of The Lorain County University Center Partnership Plan was conceived. In chapter 11, Marcia J. Ballinger and John R. Crooks detail the multiple partners, programs, practices, and promises from Lorain County Community College's successful and sustainable collaborations.

Andrew K. Koch and John N. Gardner advance a committed, enthusiastic view of a comprehensive community college baccalaureate in chapter 12. They endorse the student success–centered philosophy of community colleges and the access these students have for remedial work, should it be needed, and advocate for a model institution that provides support for students through the bachelor's degree. They are in effect bringing to the table a new concept for a college—the "comprehensive college."

We invite you as a reader to allow these contributors to help you suspend your categorical thinking and get unstuck.

Reference

Paquet, G. (2006). *Savoirs, savoir-faire, savoir-être: In praise of professional wroughting and wrighting. A think-piece prepared for Campus 2020—an inquiry into the future of British Columbia's postsecondary education system.* Victoria (BC): Ministry of Advanced Education. Available at http://gouvernance.ca/publications/06-18.pdf.

PART ONE

NEEDS, IMPLICATIONS, AND POLITICS

THE HISTORY OF THE COMMUNITY COLLEGE BACCALAUREATE MOVEMENT

Meeting the Educational Needs of the 21st Century

Kenneth P. Walker and Edith Pendleton

This chapter describes the history and role of the Community College Baccalaureate Association (CCBA) in the context of the community college baccalaureate movement. This movement has guided bold and creative pathways to baccalaureate attainment for those historically disenfranchised from higher education. The CCBA Board of Directors has encouraged all models that enhance access to baccalaureate programs, including bachelor's degrees awarded by community/state colleges, articulation agreements with universities, shaping distance learning affiliations, and improving the awareness of university centers as points of access.

Historic Overview

At the core of the American Dream is the assumption that all citizens deserve an equal opportunity to earn a college degree. "If a nation expects to be ignorant and free, in a state of civilization," Thomas Jefferson wrote in 1816, "it expects what never was and never will be" (Jefferson, 1816).

In 1847, Townsend Harris convinced New York City's Board of Education to found the Free Academy, later renamed the City College of New York, to provide higher education to its burgeoning population of immigrants and laborers. "Open the doors to all—let the children of the rich and poor take seats together and know no distinction save that of industry, good conduct, and intellect," Harris urged (Bremner, 1974, p. 1941).

Such egalitarian statesmen realized that the success of our society depends on the nation's ability to "help all citizens become functioning, self-governing members of the republic" (Christensen, Horn, & Johnson, 2008, p. 52). A knowledge-based society that neglects its education system forfeits its intellectual superiority and social advantage to competitors.

The Morrill Act of 1862 established land grant universities, known as industrial colleges, to educate the working class in such fields as teaching, animal husbandry, and mechanical arts. Their practical mission was further reinforced by the Hatch Act of 1887, which established agricultural research stations to study and disseminate means of enhancing food production. These federal actions heralded the creation of the applied baccalaureate.

Despite efforts to accelerate America's shift from an agrarian to an industrial economy, by 1940 only 34% of young adults held a high school diploma, and only 6% had a bachelor's degree (U.S. Department of Commerce, Economics and Statistics Administration, Bureau of the Census, 1994, para. 5). Social tensions aroused by race and gender bias accentuated the inequities of higher education. As Thomas N. Bonner explains it:

> The vast changes that crumbled the ivory tower of 1940 were not only unforeseen and unplanned, but were largely unintended and sometimes unwanted. Educators did not control developments but were carried along on the swift social and demographic currents that washed over their hermetic little world—the demands of war, returning veterans, international crises, economic growth, the baby boom, political strife, Vietnam, campus revolt, economic decline and changing public support. (1986, p. 44)

The Serviceman's Readjustment Act of 1944 (The GI Bill of Rights) afforded thousands of World War II veterans "the opportunity of resuming their education or technical training, after discharge, or of taking a refresher or re-trainer course, not only without tuition charge up to $500 per school year, but with the right to receive a monthly living allowance while pursuing their studies" (Roosevelt, 1944, para. 1). "Almost overnight, the GI Bill changed our ideas about who should go to college. The example set by the veterans changed the expectations of others, . . . many of whom now began to think of college as something within their grasp" (Bonner, 1986, p. 47). Economists and historians credit the bill with inspiring entrepreneurial prosperity as millions of veterans attained a college degree and took up leadership roles in business.

Three years later, the Truman Commission Report recommended that "the number of community colleges be increased," and that these "serve as an instrument of social transition" (U.S. President's Commission on Higher Education, 1947, Vol. 1, p. 6). The Commission wrote, "Some community colleges may offer a full four years of college work, but most of them probably will stop at the end of . . . the sophomore year" (p. 67).

Accessible to all, these colleges would remove religious and racial barriers and provide generous financial aid. "The discovery, training, and utilization of individual talents is of fundamental importance in a free society. To liberate and perfect the intrinsic powers of every citizen is the central purpose of democracy, and its furtherance of individual self-realization is its greatest glory" (U.S. President's Commission on Higher Education, p. 9). "By allowing the opportunity for higher education to depend so largely on the individual's economic status, we are not only denying to millions of young people the chance in life to which they are entitled; we are also depriving the Nation of a vast amount of potential leadership and potential social competence which it sorely needs" (p. 29).

For a nation emboldened by military success, the practical appeal of the associate in science degree and its promise of prosperity propelled rapid expansion of the community college system. Managed by their individual states, these responsive, innovative institutions received funding based on student enrollment and completion rates.

By the early 1990s, many community colleges began sidelining costly liberal arts curricula to capitalize on incentives such as the Carl D. Perkins Vocational and Applied Technology Education Act of 1990, which subsidized cooperative programs between secondary schools and community colleges that prepared students for the workforce. University-transfer enrollments declined as students sought terminal degrees that catapulted them into high wage employment within two years of enrollment. The proliferation of workforce programs, frequently designed and taught by industry practitioners, fortified the perception of community colleges as vocational centers that catered to students unable to meet the rigorous admissions requirements of state universities. In keeping with the open-door mission, community colleges were compelled to serve a growing ratio of underprepared students who required labor-intensive remediation. As Edmund J. Gleazer Jr. observed, "One would think that schools, community colleges, and universities would have the most natural of connections as learners move through them in the formal education process. All too often, that is not the case. Students seem obliged to jump from pool to pool rather than finding themselves in a continuing stream" (1980, p. 11).

Educators nationwide began advocating for creative solutions, arguing that traditional thinking, based on past experiences, limited by turf protection and personal interests, does a disservice to the millions of students who need a baccalaureate degree, but can't attend a university. The benefits of expanding the capacity and reach of the community college system seemed self-evident. Authorizing community colleges to offer baccalaureate degrees would include the following benefits:

Increase geographical, financial, and academic access to higher education.

Promote cost efficiencies by using existing infrastructure.

Maximize human resources, for example, hire community college faculty qualified to teach upper division courses.

Support success among nontraditional or returning students through smaller classes, less rigid sequencing, and greater scheduling options.

Promote ready articulation and upward mobility for students with associate degrees.

Provide for cooperative use of community facilities for work-based learning.

Maintain students' family and employment relationships while completing a degree.

Expand community college commitment to economic development.

Respond to community needs for specialized programs.

The applied baccalaureate degrees employers seek are often unavailable at state universities that traditionally invest their intellectual capital in research and graduate study, and are poorly prepared to deliver training in such technical occupations as computer science, public safety management, prosthetics, radiographic technology and physical therapy. Community colleges, on the other hand, are ideally suited to expand and build on existing associate of science programs in these groundbreaking fields.

The world's critical reliance on technology has profoundly altered the definition of an educated workforce, provoking far-reaching disruption to pedagogies and best practices, testing the ingenuity and capacity of higher education to embrace the rich array of possibilities afforded by global integration. As previously unimagined professions emerge and mature, levels of

intellect and sophistication required in those fields go well beyond the training needed in the past, further clouding the distinction between learning for
intellectual development and effective citizenship as opposed to acquiring of
skills for gainful employment.

In 1997, the Commission on National Investment in Higher Education's
report, "Breaking the Social Contract: The Fiscal Crisis in Higher Education," predicted that budget shortfalls could force the nation's colleges and
universities to deny access to thousands of qualified students. The report
described "a time bomb ticking under the nation's social and economic
foundations: At a time when the level of education needed for productive
employment is increasing, the opportunity to go to college will be denied to
millions of Americans unless sweeping changes are made to control costs,
halt sharp increases in tuition, and increase other sources of revenue" (p. 6).

Thus the logic, economic effectiveness, and ease of implementation of
the baccalaureate degree at the community college began to gain acceptance
as a commonsense solution to the problems of increasing demand, limited
access, and rising cost in higher education. The tide clearly turned when, in
2000, the Carnegie Foundation for the Advancement of Teaching added a
hybrid category of baccalaureate colleges to the Carnegie Classification, the
"Baccalaureate/Associate's College," for colleges primarily conferring associate's degrees, but with at least 10% at the baccalaureate level (2001).

The Community College Baccalaureate Movement

Authorization to award community college baccalaureate degrees came
through isolated legislative initiatives, first in New York (1970), then Texas
(1985), Utah and Vermont (1993), Arkansas and Florida (1997), and Nevada
(1998) (CCBA Executive Director Beth Hagan, personal communication,
February 25, 2011). These pioneering applied baccalaureate degrees filled
industrial needs such as manufacturing technology and were meant to fortify
the nation's workforce without compromising scholastic rigor.

Founded in 1999, the Community College Baccalaureate Association
proved an effective, influential advocacy organization whose current members include representatives from 25 states, 5 Canadian provinces, and the
United Kingdom, Denmark, South Africa, India, Australia, Japan, among
others.

In August of 1998, the North Central Association of Colleges and
Schools Commission on Institutions of Higher Education received its first
request from a community college to extend its accreditation to a few

competency-based programs leading to a bachelor of applied technology. Dr. Steven Crow, executive director of the Commission on Institutions of Higher Education at the time, and Dr. Doreen Dailey, then president of Yavapai Community College in Prescott, Arizona, served on the Task Force on Baccalaureate Education in the Community College Setting, and spoke at the CCBA's first annual conference in February 2001, attended by representatives of 17 states, 2 Canadian provinces, and 2 Caribbean nations ("North Central Association Publishes," 2001). Participants identified strategies to accelerate widespread acceptance of the community college baccalaureate degree, including:

> Elicit backing of like-minded organizations, such as the American Association of Community Colleges and the Association of Community College Trustees.
> Organize approach to regional accrediting agencies.
> Establish lines of communication with state departments of education and higher education boards.
> Target efforts toward key states where initiatives have gained momentum.
> Encourage graduate research on community college baccalaureate degrees.

"We developed an 'Of Like Minds' initiative in 2004 to leverage the resources of other associations with CCBA to achieve our respective missions that are so similar in many ways," reported CCBA Executive Director Beth Hagan (personal correspondence, March 4, 2011). These included the League for Innovation, National Institute for Staff and Organizational Development, the National Association of Community College Teacher Education Programs (NACCTEP), National Council for Workforce Education, and the Hispanic Association of Colleges and Universities. The groups share press releases, attend each other's conferences without cost and, in the case of NACCTEP, share our conferences' opening reception.

Then in 2005, 12 scholars joined in publishing the first in-depth book on the subject, *The Community College Baccalaureate: Emerging Trends and Policy Issues* (Floyd, Skolnik, & Walker, 2005). Brisk sales confirmed a growing interest in the views of proponents and critics on the subject.

Over the last decade, members of the movement have constructed a pliable framework for higher education that responds to the needs of students and the labor market, fulfilling its mission to "promote better access to the baccalaureate degree on community college campuses, and to serve as a resource for information on various models for accomplishing this purpose" (CCBA, 2010). Its annual meetings continue to provide a climate of meaningful discussion about policies and practices that ensure students will receive the preparation necessary for success. In 2006–2007, community colleges awarded more than 500 bachelor's degrees.

According to a 2006 Pappas Consulting Group's study, only about one in five Floridians held a college degree. The report indicated the state's economy would suffer for want of an educated workforce and suggested that Florida create a tiered system of higher education, with some institutions concentrating on producing bachelor's degrees and some universities focusing on research and graduate programs.[1]

The CCBA continued to serve as a convener and catalyst for community college practitioners interested in issues of access. By spring 2006, three of Canada's four largest provinces had authorized community colleges to offer the baccalaureate degree, serving emerging fields beyond our imagination just 20 years ago.

Similar forces influenced the evolution of the applied baccalaureate in Canada. "Alberta colleges began offering a limited number of applied baccalaureate degrees in 1995 as part of a slow, deliberate, six-year trial" that ensured "careful planning, formative assessment, and thoughtful implementation" (Skolnik, 2005, p. 10) in direct response to the needs of students in applied career education.

> The Ontario colleges of applied arts and technology were designed to perform a predominantly economic role. Their main job—originally, and to this day—has been to prepare workers for the provincial economy, particularly workers in the middle of the occupational hierarchy. To support their occupational education function, the colleges developed capabilities in general education and developmental education. As the middle level occupations for which the colleges were intended to provide entry level education have evolved, college curricula, programs and resources for educating practitioners in these fields have evolved correspondingly. (Skolnik, 2005, p. 7)[2]

Sound scholarly research emanating from university practitioners and academicians proved not only influential but pivotal in encouraging the emergence of the applied baccalaureate. As D. L. Floyd observed, "While community colleges have a rich history of pragmatically leading innovative practices, all too often practitioners are too busy leading change to document their innovations in writing. University professors specializing in the study of community colleges have played key roles in nurturing and documenting innovative changes by encouraging field based research, publishing journal articles, guiding doctoral dissertation research, and serving as consultants to college leaders addressing challenges of change" (personal communication, February 9, 2009).

National studies have continued to emphasize the need for dramatic changes in education at all levels. For example, researchers at the Institute for Higher Education Policy concluded in 2007, "There is no major postsecondary institution, program, or policy in the world with a specific focus on addressing the issues rising out of the new world economic and demographic order which is emerging around us" (2007, p. 37). They recommended the establishment of "a new kind of four-year postsecondary institution—one that can address the complex historical, economic, political, sociological, ecological, and entrepreneurial forces which are reshaping the world as we know it and challenging the ability of individuals to attain the American dream of prosperity and civic enlightenment. This new institution could serve as a model for a new kind of university in the 21st century . . . global in outlook but local in its delivery, . . . using the knowledge of the best minds available to bring practical solutions to a population struggling with the dramatic shift from an agricultural to an industrial society" (p. 37).

Founding of the *Journal of the New Comprehensive College* in 2008 provided an invigorating forum for shared experiences and best practices about improving access to baccalaureate degrees while encouraging research relevant to the mission of the CCBA. That year, the Lumina Foundation for Education invited 115 higher education and workforce experts to discuss "Applied Baccalaureate Developments and Future Implications" and means of enhancing degree completion for working adults. To capture the authentic voices of students affected by the movement, the CCBA launched a student essay contest in 2002, offering a cash prize to winners. A compilation of these inspiring personal narratives was published in 2011. In 2010, the CCBA affiliated with Golden Key Honor Society, offering students in baccalaureate-conferring community colleges access to scholarships, leadership training, and participation in conferences.

The Digital Age

In the coming years, proprietary, charter, and e-colleges will pose fresh challenges to the survival of the public community college as its mission matures to meet the changing dynamics of the communities it serves.

It is an economic reality that education and income are inextricably linked.

> As service related jobs have come to dominate the workplace, the college degree—or at least some form of postsecondary education and training—has replaced the high school diploma as the entry card into rewarding employment. . . . Unless the nation makes a concerted effort to raise the level of education and skill of these Americans, the wage disparity between the rich and the poor will become so large that it will threaten both America's social stability and its core democratic values. Widespread access to higher education is therefore critical to the economic health and social welfare of the nation (Commission on National Investment in Higher Education, Council for Aid to Education, & Rand Corporation, 1997, p. 6.)

As advances in the Internet further transform knowledge into a marketable commodity, students become informed consumers prepared to negotiate for high-quality, low-cost college alternatives and transferable credits that can be banked and applied toward a degree anywhere in the world. The further dissolution of geographic boundaries dividing school and college districts and virtual students from their professors continues to provoke a reexamination of the principles undergirding the hierarchy of higher education.

Notes

1. For the last decade, the state of Florida has spearheaded the legislative effort to authorize community college baccalaureate degrees. The creation of the Florida College System in 2008 confirmed the merits and value of the community based baccalaureate in providing cost effective, accessible, and affordable four-year degrees. For a detailed discussion, see chapter 7, by Floyd and Falconetti.

2. For further discussion on the development and state of the community college baccalaureate in Canada, see Skolnik's chapter (chapter 9) in this book.

References

Bonner, Thomas N. (1986). The unintended revolution in America's colleges since 1940. *Change,* September/October, 44–51.

Bremner, R. H. (Ed.). (1974). *Children and youth in America: A documentary history.* Vol. 3, p. 1,941. Cambridge, MA: Harvard University Press.

Carl D. Perkins Vocational and Applied Technology Education Act of 1990 and Amendments of 1998, Pub. L. No. 105–332, 112 Stat. 3076 (1998).

Carnegie Foundation for the Advancement of Teaching. (2001). *The Carnegie classification of institutions of higher education: A technical report.* Menlo Park, CA: Carnegie Publications.

Christensen, C. M., Horn, M. B., & Johnson, C. W. (2008). *Disrupting class: How disruptive innovation will change the way the world learns.* New York, NY: McGraw Hill.

Commission on National Investment in Higher Education, Council for Aid to Education, & Rand Corporation. (1997). *Breaking the social contract: The fiscal crisis in higher education.* Retrieved from http://www.eric.ed.gov/PDFS/ED414806.pdf

Community College Baccalaureate Association. (2010). "Philosophy, Purpose, Mission." Retrieved from http://www.accbd.org

Floyd, D., Skolnik, M., & Walker, K. (Eds.). (2005). The community college baccalaureate: Emerging trends & policy issues. Sterling, VA: Stylus.

Gleazer, E. J., Jr. (1980). *The community college: Values, vision, and vitality.* Washington, DC: American Association of Community and Junior Colleges.

Institute for Higher Education Policy. (2007). *Improving access to bachelor's degrees in Macomb County* (Report). Retrieved from state of Michigan website: http://www.michigan.gov/documents/gov/Macomb_County_IHEP_Report_193846_7.pdf

Jefferson, T. (January 6, 1816). [Letter to Colonel Charles Yancy]. In P. L. Ford (Ed.). (1899). *The writings of Thomas Jefferson* (Vol. 10, p. 4). New York, NY: G. P. Putnam's Sons.

Morrill Act of 1862, 7 U.S.C. § 301 (1862).

"North Central Association Publishes Task Force Recommendations." (2001, Spring/Summer). *CCBA Beacon.* Retrieved from http://www.accbd.org/wp-content/uploads/2010/08/v2-no2.pdf

Roosevelt, F. D. (1944). *Statement on signing the G.I. Bill.* Retrieved from http://www.docstoc.com/docs/53084273/Franklin-Roosevelt-Statement-on-Signing-the-G

Servicemen's Readjustment Act of 1944, Pub. L. No. 78–346, 58 Stat. 284m (1944).

Skolnik, M. L. (2005, January). *Why Ontario universities should welcome the academic enhancement of the colleges of applied arts and technology.* Paper presented at conference of the Ontario Confederation of University Faculty Associations, Toronto, ON. Retrieved from http://ocufa.on.ca/wordpress/assets/Michael-Skolnik.pdf

U.S. Department of Commerce, Economics and Statistics Administration, Bureau of the Census. (1994). *Census questionnaire content, 1990 CQC-13.* Retrieved from http://www.census.gov/apsd/cqc/cqc13.pdf

U.S. President's Commission on Higher Education. (1947). *Higher education for democracy.* Washington, DC: Government Printing Office.

2

THE COMMUNITY COLLEGE BACCALAUREATE
Process and Politics

Linda M. Thor and Chris Bustamante

In most instances, obtaining authorization to offer the community college baccalaureate degree requires state legislative approval. When Rio Salado College challenged the status quo by seeking such approval from the Arizona State legislature, a political firestorm erupted over issues of mission, need, and cost. A heated battle ensued between this public Maricopa community college and several of its public and private university competitors. The controversial issue was played out through legislative hearings, in the media, and behind the scenes for the next eight years. Although the legislative effort was ultimately unsuccessful, the goal of increased access has progressed in Arizona as a result of bringing attention to the need for more baccalaureate options and pathways. In this chapter, we will present Rio Salado's experience as a case study along with strategies and lessons learned.

The origins of Rio Salado College's attempt to gain approval for the community college baccalaureate can be traced to the State of Arizona's legislative session beginning in January 1997. At the time, Linda Thor and Chris Bustamante were serving, respectively, as president of Rio Salado College and as a seasoned lobbyist for the Maricopa Community College District, the largest district of its type in the nation in terms of head count.

Before proceeding with the specifics of the battle for the baccalaureate, it is worthwhile to review the statewide catalysts that led to the call for higher education change and to note the political climate of those times.

Arizona's Catalysts for Change

For decades, Arizona has ranked as one of the nation's top five fastest growing states, with a rapidly decreasing median age. According to U.S. Census
data, between 1990 and 2000 Arizona's population grew from 3,665,228 to
5,130,632, the 5th-largest increase and 2nd-largest percentage gain (40%)
among the 50 states. In spite of this soaring growth, during the 1990s the
state had fewer higher educational options per capita than comparably sized
states.

In addition to the community college system, the public higher education system was built around three state universities—Arizona State University (ASU) in Tempe, a suburb of Phoenix; University of Arizona (UA) in
Tucson; and Northern Arizona University (NAU) in Flagstaff. The courses
and degree programs at these institutions were still targeted largely at the 18-
to 25-year-old population. There were limited evening and weekend classes.
This was inadequate to address the specific needs of working adults, namely,
rotating work schedules; commuting; juggling work, home, and studies; and
the need to constantly upgrade professional knowledge. However, Arizona's
extensive rural populations were only accommodated by public university
extension centers or distance learning. The smaller private universities that
did exist tended to be highly specialized, such as Embry Riddle Aeronautical
University in the Prescott area, or they were branches of institutions head-
quartered elsewhere, such as Ottawa University. The exception, of course, is
the mega University of Phoenix (UOP).

In contrast, there were 19 Arizona community colleges. Collectively they
served in excess of 200,000 students—more than the public universities
combined. However, Arizona's community colleges did and still do receive
significantly less state funding per student than the three state universities.
They were and are primarily funded through property-tax revenue and
tuition. At approximately $450 a semester for a full-time student, tuition in
1997 was just over half that of the state universities. In recent years, the
community colleges have faced record student-enrollment increases. The
largest district in the state is the Maricopa Community College system, with
its 10 colleges: Chandler-Gilbert, Estrella Mountain, Gateway, Glendale,
Mesa, Paradise Valley, Phoenix, Rio Salado, Scottsdale, and South Mountain. Arizona's rural colleges are Arizona Western, Central Arizona, Cochise,
Coconino, Eastern, Mohave, Northland Pioneer, Pima, and Yavapai.

As is true today, the line between two-year and four-year colleges had
become increasingly blurred. Nationally, studies indicated that on average it

took a student up to four years to earn a so-called "two-year" degree and up to seven years to earn a "four-year," or bachelor's degree. The reasons varied. As tuition increased, students found it necessary to limit course loads. And, as more adults entered the higher education system, they needed to balance work and family life with studies. Noting this trend, the *New York Times* stated, "In ways legislators in state capitols and in Washington are struggling to make sense of, the higher education mainstream is coming to look a lot more like Rio Salado and Maricopa than like Harvard or Yale" (Applebome, 1997, pp. 24–26).

The 1997 Legislative Session: Senate Bill 1109 Introduces a New Model of Higher Education

With all these catalysts in place, the time appeared right for introducing new models that would revolutionize access to higher education in Arizona. It was in this climate, just prior to the 1997 Arizona legislative session, that Carol Springer, a powerful Republican, who served in the Arizona State Senate from 1990 to 1998, set the community college baccalaureate movement in motion. Senator Springer was the Appropriations chair, and this gave her a great vantage point from which to push for this change, because she had great influence on the purse strings of the state's public universities and community colleges. Her constituents resided in the rural areas surrounding the town of Prescott, and she recognized their unmet educational needs. Her initial bill was simply a request to appropriate $940,000 to aid an existing cooperative program between Northern Arizona University and Yavapai College in Prescott.

Shortly thereafter, she approached the Maricopa Community Colleges with a broader plan: Senate Bill (SB) 1109, which would authorize the community college baccalaureate. She had learned of similar models across the nation and in surrounding states with rural populations, such as Utah and Nevada. Implementing such a change would require the legislature to delete just four words in the statute authorizing community colleges. The Maricopa chancellor, Dr. Paul Elsner, was favorably inclined. He was nationally acknowledged as a visionary throughout his lengthy career with the Maricopa Community Colleges. In assessing the legislation's potential for the state's community colleges, he realized that the one most likely to grasp the concept and successfully implement it in short order was the very nontraditional Rio Salado. The college was not restricted by the usual geographic service boundaries. Established in 1978 as a "college without walls," it was never intended to have a large physical campus. Rather it brought quality, flexible college courses to working adults, using distance learning formats and in-person programs at major employers and in community centers.

In early 1997, Rio Salado served some 34,000 students annually, making it the third largest in head count of the 10 Maricopa Community Colleges. The 1996–1997 academic year was a pivotal one for Rio Salado for several reasons. First, during that time Rio Salado became the first college or university in the Southwest to offer courses online, backed up by placing the college's entire student support services online as well. Immediately, student enrollment began to surge, with a corresponding increase in full-time student equivalents (FTSEs). Within the next 10 years, online offerings would grow to more than 500 courses and more than 30,000 online students annually. The growth and popularity of online learning at Rio, combined with several highly innovative programs, qualified Rio Salado to be a major provider for the community college baccalaureate.

The Rio Salado College Applied Baccalaureate Model

One of the themes that we would stress in legislative testimonies over multiple years was that the community college baccalaureate was a model whose time had come. The concept proposed by Senator Springer was an excellent fit for the nontraditional Rio Salado. First, its focus would be on applied programs rather than theory-based programs offered by universities. The designated programs would offer advanced education and technical skills for specialized employment in communities already served by the college, which enrolled students statewide. The four applied career fields that were ultimately selected were public safety, allied health, computer technology, and business. A few years later, teacher education would be added to the mix.

Secondly, the community college baccalaureate and Rio Salado were a perfect fit because it would use Rio's expertise in distance learning formats to reach students unable to access baccalaureate degrees because of geographic barriers. This would keep local students residing as taxpayers within their own Arizona communities, saving them the cost of relocating or time-consuming commutes.

Next, the community college baccalaureate would not compete with state university programs for students. The legislation would permit these degrees only in select career fields and "workforce-related disciplines," where degrees were not currently offered by one of the state universities. In addition, the applied baccalaureate degrees offered and conferred through Rio Salado would be delivered with full articulation to Arizona's other community colleges. As an example, in 1997 there was no career pathway at the three state universities for public safety personnel through a bachelor in applied science degree in either public safety or police science. Yet Rio Salado had already served more than 10,000 police and public safety officers over the course of the decade through specialized courses and its law enforcement technology program, leading to the associate in applied science degree. A more highly educated police force would greatly benefit all Arizona communities. Several prominent chiefs within the police community would ultimately join forces with Rio Salado in the bid for the applied baccalaureate.

Another very appealing feature of the applied baccalaureate was that it would provide an alternative means to address workforce shortages. For example, there were documented shortages of highly qualified dental hygienists when the Arizona Dental Association (AzDA) approached Rio Salado for educational remedies back in the mid-1990s. With the financial support and long-term commitment of AzDA and its member dentists, the college opened the Rio Salado School of Dental Hygiene in 1998, offering an accelerated 15-month program, leading to the associate in applied science degree. Still there was no statewide equivalent baccalaureate program for articulation.

The financial plan behind SB 1109 was that applied baccalaureate students would pay "university" tuition for upper-division courses. A critical factor that would become a legislative point of contention was that no additional state funds would be required beyond those already allocated to the community colleges. In addition, supporters of the bill were emphatic that no additional faculty or physical facilities would be required. Instead, Rio Salado was highly qualified and fully prepared to offer distance-learning options for applied baccalaureate programs, most notably through online learning. These formats would effectively use existing resources, both human and tangible.

The 1997 Legislative Arguments for and Against the Community College Baccalaureate

The need to approach the Arizona legislature for a statute change was driven by the necessity to remove four simple words from the definition of *community college*. The definition would be amended as such: " 'Community college' means an educational institution which is under the jurisdiction of the state board and which provides a program of training in the arts, sciences, and humanities beyond the 12th grade of the public or private high school course of study of vocational education . . ." (SB 1109, 1997).

From the time it was introduced to legislators, Arizona's version of the community college baccalaureate created a firestorm of controversy. We were called upon multiple times to testify on behalf of SB 1109. Our testimony made it clear that this bill would enable our community colleges to do what we do best: be fully responsive to the needs of working adults and their employers. The curriculum and degrees would be designed in close partnership with the community and local employers. Other "pro" lobbying arguments we presented included:

> The mission of community colleges would not change: We did not seek to become research institutions.
>
> Applied baccalaureates would be customized for adults in ways university programs were not.
>
> Industry experts with current market experience, as opposed to full-time research professors, would teach classes.
>
> Arizona's public universities were overflowing with students and were reaching capacity.
>
> The universities had education "gaps" that community colleges could fill more cost effectively.
>
> Community colleges have always been a much more cost-effective alternative when it comes to educating.
>
> Despite articulation agreements, students were often finding that their community college credits were not accepted at the state universities.
>
> Students would receive more choices for lower-cost options.
>
> The middle class was being squeezed out of the higher education system because of cost.
>
> Rural communities could "grow their own," if their residents received their education in their own backyard.
>
> Rural students and working adults would receive better and improved access.
>
> Mothers with children, mortgages, and jobs needed more higher education options, because they cannot simply "pick up" and go off somewhere else to finish their degrees.

The issue began to receive extensive local and eventually national media coverage because then-president of Rio Salado, Linda Thor, wrote a guest column for the *Arizona Republic* called "Workforce Needs Community College Baccalaureate Degree," (Thor, 1997, p. B4) explaining how our curriculum and degrees are community driven. On the positive side, *Tribune Newspapers*—the region's second-largest circulation newspaper chain—ran an editorial that asked "Why didn't somebody think of this before?" (Editorial Staff, 1996, p. A12). A *Tribune* guest commentary by Sam Steiger, a former five-term member of Congress, appeared with the headline "Universities Standing in Way of Progress to Protect Their Turf." He wrote, "The simple truth is that the 43,000-student ASU is riddled with the tyranny of a few elitists who prefer to publish rather than teach. UA is equally dedicated to preserving and expanding its student population at the expense of teaching value" (Steiger, 1997, p. A9).

The "con" arguments against the applied baccalaureate by the university lobbyists included:

Mission erosion: That is, community colleges would depart from their core mission of providing low-cost associate degrees, workforce development, remedial and vocational education.

Mission creep: Once the community colleges received limited authority to grant applied baccalaureates, down the road they would want the same authority for academic programs.

There was simply no need and no demand for the applied baccalaureate.

There would be hidden costs and the legislature would have to produce additional funding.

It would lead to a three-tier system in which minorities and low-income students came out short.

Community colleges and their faculty members were not qualified to offer or teach baccalaureates classes.

It would undercut the existing 2 + 2 programs between public universities and community colleges.

It would lead to duplication of educational services that could lead to increased tuition.

Physical expansion would be required.

The universities had already greatly expanded their capacity to meet Arizona's needs.

The change in higher education would be too radical.

Joining the university lobbyists in opposition was the head of the Arizona Tax Research Association (ATRA), an organization that has made it a perpetual mission to oppose every single tax increase in Arizona. It should be emphasized that although SB 1109 specifically did not call for new taxes or state allocations, the ATRA representative claimed that would be an end result.

Midway through the 1997 legislative session, an editorial in *The Arizona Republic* was headlined "The Universities' Job" and declared "this well-meaning proposal is perilous for both the state's universities and its community colleges." The same article concluded the applied baccalaureate was "divisive and unneeded" (Editorial Staff, 1997, p. B6). At another point, Senator Springer was quoted in *Tribune Newspapers* as saying her bill was causing "heartburn" for the universities (Noyes, 1997, p. A1).

The Outcome of the 1997 Proposed Applied Baccalaureate Legislation

Nevertheless, SB 1109 was passed 22-8 by the Arizona Senate before its defeat in the House Education Committee. The final bullets were delivered in person through appearances by the three public university presidents: Clara Lovett of NAU, Manuel Pacheco of UA, and Lattie Coor of ASU. They argued that SB 1109 was well intentioned but misguided and needed much more study. Therefore, the House Education Committee complied by adopting an amendment to set up a committee to study the issue (Staff, 1997). It was well known that then-Governor Fife Symington was squarely against the community college baccalaureate, and he vetoed the amended bill, stating it "represents a substantial departure from the existing structure of higher education in Arizona" (Van der Werf, 1997, p. B7).

Senator Springer was equally outspoken. The *Arizona Republic* quoted her as saying, "This bill was absolutely not judged on its merits, period." She added that it was vetoed because the state's universities feared competition from community colleges (Van der Werf, 1997, pp. B1–B2).

But the movement did not end there. The legislature proceeded to form its own Higher Education Study Committee, with 13 members, including Senator Springer, representatives of major universities and the community colleges, the Arizona Board of Regents, the Arizona Community College Association, the Governor's Office, and key legislators. Linda Thor served as one of the two community college members. Among the committee's responsibilities was to determine unmet higher education baccalaureate needs, identify options, and develop specific recommendations for meeting those needs. The committee was to also research nontraditional delivery needs for career or technical fields, articulation options, possibilities for community colleges and universities to coordinate and cooperate, a cost analysis, and models for the community college baccalaureate in other states.

Months later, the committee reached consensus that the Arizona Board of Regents and the Board of Directors for the Arizona Community College Association should jointly establish a committee to continue the collaborative process. The legislature, in a 1998 footnote, provided specific charges to the committee. Thor was once again appointed, and the committee completed their work in December 1998. The committee proposed a system for identifying and meeting needs for additional baccalaureate degrees, but was unable to reach agreement on seeking legislation to allow the baccalaureate.

As reported by *Community College Week*, "What did emerge from the panel's work, however, was a proposal that if community college officials identified a need for a baccalaureate program, they could shop it around to the universities. If none were interested in offering the program on their own or in collaboration with a two-year college, then a joint review committee would look into other options—including handing the program to community colleges" (Evelyn, 1999, p. 12).

In the same issue, Thor stated that fears of mission creep or erosion were missing the point: "I am proud to be a community college. I do not want to be a university. We're not talking about a bachelor's that has the same characteristics. Frankly, we probably need another term. We're all getting hung up on the term bachelor's rather than talking about how community colleges meet certain needs" (Evelyn, 1999, p. 13).

During 1998, the applied baccalaureate issue attracted the attention of the *Chronicle of Higher Education*, which referred to it as "a landmark plan," emphasized its "practitioner" approach, and raised important issues about the overall nature of baccalaureate degrees. Should they be practical or more holistic (Healy, 1998)?

The Revitalized 2004, 2005, and 2006 Legislative Campaigns

However, legislation would not be proposed again for six years. In spring 2004 Representative Russell Pearce (R-Mesa), the chair of the House Appropriations Committee, introduced a bill to allow community colleges to offer baccalaureate degrees in fire science, law enforcement, nursing, and teacher education in a six-year pilot. This bill was defeated in committee 9-7. However, the lawmakers left the door open to reconsider the measure at a future legislative session.

By 2005, Rio Salado was a dramatically expanded and different college than it was when the concept of the community college baccalaureate was introduced eight years prior. With credit enrollment exceeding 40,000 students annually, it was poised to emerge as the largest in head count among the Maricopa Community Colleges. This growth was fueled largely by its online offerings, which numbered more than 450 unique courses.

Working in partnership with the Maricopa District, Rio Salado was still the logical choice to advocate on behalf of all community colleges, when in the winter of 2005, the community college baccalaureate issue emerged yet again in the legislature. This time the chair of the House Higher Education Committee, Representative Laura Knaparek (R-Tempe), proposed House Bill 2079. It had the ardent support of several powerful legislators, including once again the House Appropriations Committee chair, Representative Pearce. Under the bill, approximately half of Arizona's community colleges would be allowed to issue the baccalaureate, primarily in teaching, health professions, fire science, and law enforcement. However, it was understood that with the exception of Rio Salado, most of the colleges were not positioned to offer all four career paths.

The legislation proposed by Representative Knaparek would have changed how the state funds Arizona's universities and maximize use of the community college system for increased access. The funding, she stated, would follow the students, rather than the traditional "arbitrary formula where dollars are doled out by political whim instead of need" (Knaparek, 2005, p. B5).

The legislation was bolstered by positive and widespread media coverage. In advance of the legislative session, the conservative *Daily News-Sun*, serving residents of the retirement communities surrounding Sun City, issued an opinion column with the headline "Community College Bill Makes Sense." It began: "One of several disappointments by the Legislature last session was its failure to pass a sensible bill that would have allowed community colleges to begin offering four year degrees in select fields . . ." (Editorial Staff, 2004, p. A6). The *Arizona Republic*, which had been so opposed in 1997, challenged and chastised legislators, stating, "OK, skeptics, you axed university reform; now it's your turn for some new ideas (Editorial Staff, February 16, 2005, p. B6). Another editorial in the *East Valley Tribune* touted, "4-Year Community College Degrees Deserve a Try" (Editorial Staff, December 2, 2005, p. A20).

An additionally encouraging sign was an independent statewide public opinion poll, which found that 74% of those surveyed would support a bill "that would allow community colleges to offer four-year baccalaureate degrees" (Merrill, 2005).

We again returned with our supporters to the legislative chambers with our messages of access, affordability, specialization, economic efficiency, experience, and this time, widespread support. We cited U.S. Census statistics indicating that Arizona ranks 20th in population with 3 public universities. In contrast, Maryland, ranking 19th in population, has 14 public universities, and Minnesota, ranking 21st in population, has 14 public universities. We told legislators how Rio Salado's 10,600 occupational certificates and degrees in 2004 accounted for 76% of the total awards presented that year. We were pleased to report that the accrediting body for Arizona's community colleges and three public universities—the Higher Learning Commission of the North Central Association—had concluded that these degrees would not compromise the community colleges' traditional mission.

But once again, HB 2079 was met with fierce opposition from the universities, and turf wars erupted. Each committee meeting was populated by a sizable number of opposition lobbyists from both the private sector, including the UOP, and the public sector, including all three state universities. And again, the representative from ATRA was on hand, claiming that taxpayers would be left footing the bill. As always, our position was that an adjusted tuition plan would pay for the costs incurred. However, university lobbyists told the legislators that if passed, the bill would cost the state $20 million in its first year alone.

In spite of this, the bill proceeded fairly smoothly through the House and was then approved by the Senate Higher Education Committee. At this point, we were as cautiously optimistic as we had ever been. It appeared this time the applied baccalaureate just might become a reality. The final hurdle to pass the bill was the vote in the Senate Appropriations Committee, scheduled for April 5, 2005. However, before any testimony was heard, Bob Burns (R-Peoria), who chaired the Senate Appropriations Committee, told Representative Knaparek, "I don't think the bill, in its present form, will be able to make it through this committee" (Slivka, 2005, p. B1).

In a last-minute attempt to keep her legislation alive, Representative Knaparek offered an amendment that would have gutted the specifics of the bill. For instance, it would have taken out any reference to funding. That would have eliminated writing a new university funding formula into statute. Under her revision, the community colleges would have been authorized to offer baccalaureate degrees without any funding. Nevertheless, on April 5, 2005, the community college baccalaureate bill received its final legislative defeat in the Senate Appropriations Committee on a 6-5 vote. The majority sided with university lobbyists, who called for more time to study the state's higher education gaps and then determine the best way to fill them.

In spite of so many legislative committee meetings and testimonies, a previous report from an appointed Higher Education Committee, positive media messages, and community support, the cause was defeated by a single vote. In Representative Knaparek's words, "The political reality is that their lobbyists beat us." She complained that the universities feared a "more cost-efficient competitor" (Slivka, 2005, pp. B1–B2).

The rhetoric intensified within the media. "Blocking Community Colleges' 4-year Aspirations is Asinine" stated the *East Valley Tribune*, adding: "Sensible people have been asking for years why this arbitrary barrier to community colleges meeting expanding educational demands in a variety of areas persists" (Editorial Staff, April 7, 2005, p. A12).

But in an unusual twist, six days later, the baccalaureate authority was resurrected under a special legislative format as SB 1109, ultimately passing through the full House on a 31-28 vote and proceeding to the Senate, where it was once again killed. Reminiscent of years before, another study committee was convened, this one called the Joint Ad Hoc Task Force on Higher Education.

By the end of 2005, the applied baccalaureate was still receiving considerable renewed media attention. Articles in the state's largest newspapers were reporting a more positive outlook for the community college baccalaureate in Arizona. A December 19 article appeared in the *Arizona Republic* with the headline "Support for 4-Year Degrees Mounting" (Editorial Staff, December 19, 2005, p. B4).

The December 2, 2005, *East Valley Tribune* published this headline: "4-Year Community College Degrees Deserve a Try" (Editorial Staff, December 2, 2005, p. A20). The editorial called for pilot programs, while mocking a UOP-funded study that concluded the applied baccalaureate was a bad idea. The headline for another *Tribune* commentary by a Scottsdale city councilman stated, "ASU's gouging justifies 4-year community college degrees" (Lane, n.d., p. A12). The councilman pointed out that 70% tuition increases at ASU do not follow the state university mission to provide in-state instruction in a manner "as nearly free as possible."

Nevertheless, we were proud of the fact that this bill, which was characterized as higher education reform legislation, was approved by the full House and made it through its policy committee in the Senate. Although we faced heavy opposition and extensive public and behind-the-scenes lobbying by the public and private universities, we persevered because we believe that providing access to affordable, accessible baccalaureate degrees is the right thing to do for our students and our state.

Legislation for the applied baccalaureate would be sponsored one more time, in spring 2006. Representative Knaparek, still chair of the House Higher Education Committee, again introduced the bill, but it was compromised to the point that we could not support it.

To date, the 2006 Arizona legislative session has been the final one to witness sponsorship of any type of bill advocating for the community college applied baccalaureate. With the economic downturn starting in 2007, and states like Arizona scrambling to balance their budgets by slashing higher education, it is questionable if and when the issue will be addressed again through legislation.

Lessons Learned

If hindsight is always 20/20, what would we do differently from a strategic point of view?

We believe we have learned the following lessons that may help colleges in other states advance their own cause of achieving the baccalaureate.

From the start, we needed more grassroots momentum leading the charge.

Admittedly, back in 1997 we were called upon to respond on extremely short notice when we were first approached by Senator Carol Springer. The legislature was already in session. As a result, we did not have ample time to plan and execute a thoroughly organized grassroots campaign. Therefore, we advocated primarily through frequent testimony and through the supportive voices and letters of select members of the community, such as the heads of the Arizona Nursing Association and the Phoenix Law Enforcement Association.

What was also missing from our campaign was the voice of the community at large, backing up our statements that there was a great demand for these baccalaureates. The community college baccalaureate was a radical concept for people to grasp, and unfortunately, not enough people were sold on the idea. A greater volume of powerful messages from our constituents, including students and even their parents, would ideally have reinforced these messages: Arizona needs a more highly educated workforce to compete and experience economic growth. We need more options to educate our youth and working adults within our own communities, where they will then likely reside and become taxpayers. We need more highly educated police, more allied health workers, more computer technicians, and more general business graduates than the universities alone can currently provide.

Also missing was an organized movement that would present students and their parents sharing their issues of access in their own words to the legislators. Ideally, after it was organized it would be led by "the people," so the community colleges don't appear self-serving.

Unfortunately, without this grassroots momentum, our campaigns eventually fizzled. Even worse, the community colleges often appeared to be self-serving or greedy and to not have the greater community good in mind. We were inadvertently positioned as adversaries to the very popular universities. Of course, in reality the opposite was true: Our cause would greatly benefit the community through increased options that the universities were not interested in providing.

The issue of building substantial grassroots momentum did not improve in subsequent years. Legislation for the baccalaureate was not introduced during every legislative session. We typically received very brief notice when the cause was about to be revived by one or more legislators. Coupled with this short notice was the fact that in several of those years, we were also engaged in very aggressive legislative battles to retain funding for our free Adult Basic Education classes, which had grown to become the largest program of its type in Arizona. Our resources and collective energy were spread thin during those years. We had to carefully choose our battles.

We needed to attract more peer support from within the leadership ranks of Arizona's community colleges themselves.

Throughout the eight-year battle for the baccalaureate, the issue proved to be highly sensitive among members of the Chancellor's Executive Council of the Maricopa district, which consisted of the chancellor, all 10 presidents, and 4 vice-chancellors. This was understandable, because not every college stood to benefit equally from the community college baccalaureate. In fact, a number of the colleges would not initially benefit at all, simply because the model did not fit their individual mission. This contributed to Rio Salado's reputation as a renegade college.

This was particularly true back in 1997. Although the Arizona Community Colleges Presidents' Council supported SB 1109, behind the scenes some of the state's community colleges were questioning why any of us would want to offer applied baccalaureates and commenting publicly in local news media. Furthermore, support for our position was met with limited enthusiasm from our colleagues at the national level. "We are who we are," said David Pierce, then-president of the American Association of Community Colleges. "We are community-based, associate-degree-granting institutions. This [granting baccalaureate degrees] isn't necessarily our job" (Evelyn, 1999, p. 13).

> *We underestimated the collective power of the public and private universities when they unite as allies.*

As we discussed, at every legislative committee meeting, we were up against the very large, polished, and vocal contingent of unified lobbyists from the public and private universities—a sort of David and Goliath matchup. But in our case, the underdog did not always command sympathy from the majority of the legislators. In fact, our team of lobbyists was outnumbered eight to one. Also, the objections of the university lobbyists were bolstered by ATRA, which insisted that we were withholding the fact that that this was going to be a very expensive proposition for the public. The community colleges were unfairly perceived as wanting something for themselves—a type of power grab if you will—that was unnecessary. Therefore, the public and private universities came across as the ones who were truly looking out for the best interests of the general public.

> *We didn't anticipate the legislators viewing the controversy behind the applied baccalaureate among higher education entities as a "family feud."*

The university lobbyists were already well positioned and had favor with the legislators owing to the enormous local popularity of their campuses. The legislators could see merits behind both sides of the argument. Therefore, they wanted to avoid being held liable as decision makers in a very divisive debate. They wanted the universities and community colleges to work the issue out among themselves. But we could not, because the applied baccalaureate involved a change in statute.

The Rio Salado story is unique because of Arizona's political composition. Each state's political structure may call for different tactics and strategies. Issues of cost duplication and mission erosion and creep will always arise and need detailed explanations.

Subsequent Progress

As of spring 2012, there is still no community college baccalaureate in Arizona. However, we believe our cause has yielded some positive outcomes. In the absence of formal legislation, we can report that several unprecedented avenues have opened that now increase access or transferability for students across our state and outside of Arizona. For example:

> Previously the associate of applied science degree would not transfer. Now it is accepted as a block in the new baccalaureate of applied science degree at NAU, ASU Polytechnic Campus, and ASU West Campus.
>
> ASU and Rio Salado have a joint online Baccalaureate in Interdisciplinary Studies degree that transfers 75 credits from the community college.
>
> NAU accepts 90 credits from the Maricopa Community Colleges into the baccalaureate of interdisciplinary studies program.
>
> The Maricopa Community Colleges now have articulation agreements with more than 25 states and out-of-state universities that transfer between 75 and 90 community college credits.
>
> The ASU Polytechnic Campus has two Maricopa Community College partners on-site, namely, Chandler-Gilbert Community College and Mesa Community College.
>
> The nation's first communiversity west of the Mississippi opened in 2009 and features unique public–private partnerships among the City of Surprise, Rio Salado, Glendale Community College, Northern Arizona University, Phoenix College, Ottawa University, and West-MEC, a public school district specializing in vocational education
>
> A similar communiversity is under way in the Town of Queen Creek, Arizona.

On the Horizon . . . Another Opportunity?

In the seven intervening years since the bill's final defeat, much has transpired locally on the economic front. Like California and other rapidly growing states, Arizona's economy has been hit extremely hard by the economic recession. At one point the State of Arizona found itself with as much as a $6 billion budget shortfall. In an effort to balance the state's budget, higher education allocations have been drastically reduced each of the past four fiscal years.

In mid-January 2011, Arizona Governor Jan Brewer sent shock waves through the state's public higher education community by calling for even more potentially devastating budget cuts for fiscal year 2012, amounting to some $270 million. Arizona's 19 community colleges' FY 2012 state aid appropriation was impacted by a $72.9 million cut, or nearly half its funding, during the 2011 legislative session. However, equalization assistance was fully funded. Equalization assistance is state funding that is paid to community college districts that do not meet the minimum statutorily prescribed assessed valuation requirements necessary to form a district and consequently do not have the tax base sufficient to generate the revenues needed to operate the district. Equalization assistance helps to offset this shortfall.

Likewise, the FY 2012 budget for the state's three public universities cut $198 million, approximately a 40% reduction in state support from the past three years.

However, the governor, who is a community college graduate, used the crisis to call for new models of higher education. Just a few days after her call for higher education budget cuts, in a special directive to the 2011 Arizona legislature, Governor Brewer stated she wants to explore whether community colleges should be empowered to grant bachelor's degrees.

The governor told the legislature there is no way the state can financially maintain Arizona's higher education system in its present form. She called for solutions beyond the extremes of further hikes in tuition or eliminating programs. In short, she is calling for new models of higher education that will not only expand existing programs that let students start their baccalaureate degrees at community colleges, but for the creation of new four-year schools. Another option would be having additional campuses for the three public universities around the state, but with lower tuition than charged at the main campuses in Tucson, Tempe, and Flagstaff. Other options she is considering are the expansion of 2 + 2 programs. Ultimately, the governor wants to double the number of students earning baccalaureate degrees by 2020.

However, in the 2012 legislative session, no action was taken on the governor's request for the community college baccalaureate. As this chapter and book go to press, Arizona is finally expected to once again have a budget surplus in FY 2013. In spite of this news, appropriations for higher education have not improved for community colleges, and only slightly improved for universities. Although the legislature increased the state aid appropriation to the community colleges to fund increases in FTSE in FY 2013, the overall appropriation to community colleges was reduced by $5.2 million because the funding for equalization assistance declined. The universities received a net increase of just $21 million.

It is clear that the story of the community college baccalaureate in Arizona remains unfinished. Despite enduring multiple years of a housing collapse and state budget crises that mirror the national scene, Arizona emerged in the 2010 U.S. Census as the second-fastest growing state in population. Arizona is currently home to nearly 6.6 million residents, which translates into more than a 28% growth rate since the 2000 U.S. Census. In contrast, the total U.S. population recorded growth of slightly more than 9% during the same decade. Arizona, like most Western states, is growing faster than the nation as a whole. Furthermore, more than 1 out of every 4 Arizonans is under the age of 18, which also exceeds the national average, according to the U.S. Census Bureau (U.S. Census Bureau, 2011).

Faced with shrinking financial resources, the state's higher education institutions must undergo revolutionary changes to comprehensively serve two burgeoning populations: youth who will graduate from high school in the coming decade, and adults who will need to be retrained and retooled to keep pace with the state's post-recession job market. We would argue that in the foreseeable future, the only logical solution for our state is to move forward with new models of public higher education, which include the community college baccalaureate.

References

Applebome, P. (1997, August 3). Community colleges at a crossroads—Which way is up? *The New York Times,* section 4A, pp. 24–26.

Editorial Staff. (2005, December 19). Support for 4-year degrees mounting. *The Arizona Republic,* p. B4.

Editorial Staff. (2005, December 2). 4-year community college degrees deserve a try. *East Valley Tribune,* p. A20.

Editorial Staff. (2005, April 7). Craven cave-in: Blocking community colleges' 4-year aspirations is asinine. *East Valley Tribune,* p. A12.

Editorial Staff. (2005, February 16). Higher education/our stand: OK, skeptics, you axed reform; now it's your turn for some new ideas. *The Arizona Republic,* p. B6.

Editorial Staff. (2004, December 6). Community college bill makes sense. *Daily News-Sun,* p. A6.

Editorial Staff. (1997, March 19). Four-year degrees: The universities' job. *The Arizona Republic,* p. B6.

Editorial Staff. (1996, November 22). Expanding community colleges. *Tribune Newspapers,* p. A12.

Evelyn, J. (1999, August 23). The bid for the bachelor's. *Community College Week,* pp. 12–13.

Healy, P. (1998, February 27). A 2-year college in Arizona bills itself as a new model for public higher education. *The Chronicle of Higher Education,* pp. A32–A33.

Knaparek, L. (2005, March 19). Let funds follow the students. *East Valley Tribune,* p. B5.

Lane, J. (n.d.) East valley voice: ASU's gouging justifies 4-year community college degrees. *East Valley Tribune,* p. A12.

Merrill, B. (2005, February 22). *Cronkite/eight poll: Voters don't want junk food in the schools, but they do want community colleges to award four-year diplomas* (Press release). Walter Cronkite School of Journalism, Arizona State University.

Noyes, F. (1997, February 23). College bill debate continues. *Tribune Newspapers,* p. A1.

SB 1109, Ariz. Rev. Stat. §15-1401. 1st Reg. Sess. 43d Legis. (1997).

Slivka, J. (2005, April 6). College bill dies in Senate. *The Arizona Republic,* pp. B1–B2.

Staff. (1997, March 21). New degrees for 2-year colleges killed in House. *Arizona Capitol Times,* pp. 4–5.

Steiger, S. (1997, February 18). Universities standing in way of progress to protect their turf. *Tribune Newspapers,* p. A9.

Thor, L. M. (1997, April 3). Workforce needs community college baccalaureate degree. *Arizona Republic,* p. B4.

U.S. Census Bureau. (2011). *Quick Facts.* Retrieved from http://quickfacts.census gov/qfd/states/04000.html

Van der Werf, M. (1997, April 29). Study of 4-year degrees for small colleges vetoed. *The Arizona Republic,* pp. B1–B2.

3

MISSION METAMORPHOSIS

John Patrick Rice

igher education became a part of the DNA of life in rural Nevada in 1967, when Great Basin College (GBC) opened its main campus in Elko. Since that time, the school has grown to serve a 62,000-square-mile area, straddling two time zones, bordering California, Oregon, Idaho, and Utah, and populated by 127,000 people. Learning centers are located in Ely, Pahrump, and Winnemucca, with a satellite center in Battle Mountain and Tonopah and facilities in 19 communities in between. GBC's service area is larger than Rhode Island, Delaware, Connecticut, New Jersey, New Hampshire, Vermont, Massachusetts, and Maryland *combined*.

In the fall of 1999, Great Basin College began one of the most unique endeavors in the history of the Nevada System of Higher Education. Responding to the needs of its service area the two-year comprehensive community college, awarding certificates and associate degrees, began upper-division instruction aimed at awarding students with a bachelor's degree in elementary education. Great Basin College was suddenly the most remote postsecondary institution in the contiguous 48 United States accredited to award a baccalaureate degree.

But the degree program that began the democratization of higher education for rural Nevadans did not blossom overnight. First, a visionary volunteer group of faculty, representing every discipline of the school gathered to confer. Their focus was the education of their students, the growth of the institution, and the quality of life in rural Nevada. GBC was a small school, with a small faculty and a limited number of specialized disciplines. To that end, they attended to the development of an integrative program curriculum that would capitalize on the strengths of the existing faculty. In addition, the group designed an admissions process that could dovetail with the existing lower-division course work and the traditional "open admission" policy of a comprehensive community college. Perhaps most importantly, they committed to closely advising students (many of whom were first-generation college-goers) through the process of successfully completing their baccalaureate degree.

When application to the program was first advertised in 1999, dozens of students applied. In the first semester, 45 baccalaureate students were accepted. Now, early in 2012, nearly 500 students have graduated from GBC's bachelor's degree programs, including the education program, which now offers certification for secondary and special education in addition to the original elementary certification. The array of baccalaureate degrees has expanded to include: a bachelor of arts in integrative studies, with concentrations in half a dozen areas; a bachelor of applied science in three disciplines; a bachelor of science–nursing; and a 3 + 1 social work program and 2 + 2 early childhood education program with the University of Nevada, Reno, and the University of Nevada, Las Vegas, respectively, each graduating dozens of students annually. In 2011, bachelor's degrees accounted for about 14% of the college's annual awards. It was a phenomenal achievement, considering the bachelor's degree programs grew from just a good idea to an innovative example for similar institutions in just a few years. The design of the original bachelor's degree programs began as the 20th century ebbed. Subsequent programs were developed as the new millennium flowed. Faculty collaborated and designed programs blending the best elements of successful programs at other institutions with the specific needs of rural Nevada. The programs GBC offered were developed to serve students in a variety of classroom settings: from traditional live lectures to technologically and logistically complex distance education platforms, to integrative seminar sessions, combining the talents and expertise of multi-faculty teaching teams from a variety of academic disciplines.

With programs established, faculty continued to meet regularly, overseeing admissions and standards for the respective programs. The programs attracted a variety of learners, most of whom can now best be described as 21st century students, all seeking a quality education, and many requiring close advisement on topics ranging from scheduling classes to ensure efficient completion of the program, to how to juggle the responsibilities of being a good student with those of being a good mother or father or a good employee or employer. At the time, it would have been hard to find another group of faculty who worked so closely and effectively with such a diverse group of students.

Geography 101

To understand the impact of the comprehensive mission of Great Basin College, one must understand the geography of rural Nevada. Take a map of the lower 48 United States and draw a circle with a radius of 200 miles around every population center of more than 100,000 people, and you'll find just 3 places on the map where the arcs of those circles will not reach. One of them is a good portion of rural Nevada.

Serving an area with more than 600 miles separating its farthest reaches cannot be done with a lectern and a chalkboard. To do so requires Great Basin College professors and students to engage in a variety of state-of-the-art distance education technologies. In the early 1990s, GBC started delivering course work using interactive video technology. An instructor originates a class at any one of the college's campuses, and students participate in high-tech classrooms in other communities. Facilitators in the "remote" classrooms assist students with the technology. Most instructors find time during the semester to travel to every site, so students' experiences are often face-to-face. Interactive video instruction accounts for much of the enrollments generated by the college.

As the millennium approached, GBC's investment in online learning platforms increased. Now the college engages in both synchronous and asynchronous Internet instruction. Using synchronous "live-net" technologies, instructors and students meet in real time on home computers and laptops. Instructors and students communicate through real-time audio and video connections and share materials in live Internet interactions. Asynchronous Internet instruction provides even more flexibility for students. GBC's online students connect from rural towns and remote ranches, using high-speed Internet connections. A telecommunications company within the college's service area provides coverage to 96.3% of its territory. Presently, nearly 70% of those telecommunications customers subscribe to high-speed DSL. High-speed Internet connectivity will continue to grow along with satellite Internet connections and the development of 3G and 4G wireless systems. Affordable high-speed access to GBC's learning technologies and baccalaureate level instruction is now available in even the most remote of Nevada's rural communities (and throughout the nation, for that matter).

The result of GBC's engagement in distance learning technology is striking. Democratic access to higher education in rural Nevada has undergone a transformation. Great Basin College looked far beyond traditional ways of thinking about the college experience. Delivering higher education in rural Nevada has required a commitment to an inquiry of every possible way to acquire knowledge. The result is that now, *every* citizen in Nevada has access to the opportunities higher education can provide.

The transformative power of the programs and technology of Great Basin College reach beyond course work. As an example, distance learning has fostered the creation of a vast rural Nevada neighborhood. GBC could well stand for *Great Big Community*, and students from every corner of the college's enormous service area engage in conversations leading to collective projects. They link far-flung communities with a common purpose: quality of life. Faculty members tell stories illustrating the power of GBC's technological infrastructure. In one, a student from Lund, a tiny, pioneer ranching town in White Pine County in east central Nevada, discussed a challenge he was having in his community with a classmate in McDermitt, a small town closely connected to the Native American population, more than 300 miles distant, on Humboldt County's border with the state of Oregon. The student in McDermitt had already dealt with the problem, and, from her own experience, provided a solution for the young man in Lund. Two strikingly different communities—one common challenge—solved collaboratively in an interactive classroom at Great Basin College. Their diverse backgrounds combined to form a single and powerful learning experience that then radiated into and improved the quality of life in their own communities. People learn, talk, and solve problems.

For rural Nevadans, Great Basin College *is* higher education, and the new democratic access to the bachelor's degree has been a game changer for students, and especially for business and industry. In summits held with stakeholders throughout the service area, the principal challenge in every community was the recruitment and retention of professionals in disciplines ranging from health care to accounting, education to engineering. Because many prospective GBC students are place-bound (perhaps committed to their families and their family enterprises), the option of enrolling at a distant school simply may not exist. Now, with professional preparation at the bachelor's degree level available in every community in rural Nevada, professionals can be "homegrown" to serve the needs of business and industry. Graduates already residing and having a stake in their communities are now prepared to accept the professional responsibilities required to meet the business and industry needs of the service area. For students and the communities where they live, Great Basin College is not just a center for learning, but is also an instrument for enhancing the value of living in rural Nevada.

Growing Our Own

Great Basin College provides a precious human resource to the communities it serves. At the present time, rural Nevada enjoys a relatively strong economy, thanks to its tremendous gold reserves. As previously discussed, industry has difficulty recruiting and retaining professionals to serve their needs. Further, there is considerable evidence that students who study in a community will stay in a community. So, as an example, teachers and nurses educated in GBC's bachelor's degree programs then hired by rural school districts and health care facilities have stayed.

Other bachelor's programs, in agriculture, social services, resource management, and integrated studies have produced professionals who are hired in the rural communities they came from, who wish to live their lives there, raise their families, and create opportunities for generations to come.

Rural Nevadans now have the confidence that young, bachelor-prepared professionals, educated locally, will be committed to staying and advancing every aspect of their community, bringing opportunities and service to the young and to the elderly, and sharing their skills and expertise in a way that sustains and strengthens life in rural Nevada.

Democratic Access to the American Dream

The rapid advancement of the baccalaureate degree at Great Basin College has made a significant imprint on the landscape of higher education in Nevada. It can certainly be described as one of "the peoples' colleges" (Floyd & Skolnik, 2005, p. 5), because of the democratic access to higher education it has provided to rural Nevadans. Truly, though, it opens the door not only to advanced education, but to a higher quality of life. In Nevada, one of the nation's lowest-ranked states in terms of the number of citizens with a bachelor's degree, the idea of community college bachelor's degree programs has gained momentum. Since GBC pioneered the concept, other Nevada community colleges established their own select bachelor's degree programs. GBC's program design was also used as a template for the establishment of Nevada's first state college, in Henderson. It is clear that a bachelor's degree awarded by GBC is acceptable, legitimate, effective, and valuable.

What Will the Neighbors Think?

Doctors Jay Rothman and Victor Friedman wrote that there are two institutions that have effectively resisted change in the last thousand years: the Roman Catholic Church and higher education (2004). The idea of bachelor's degrees at Great Basin College was not quickly embraced. In fact, it was criticized with little or no evidence. A regular challenge to the community college baccalaureate in general, and one aimed at Great Basin College in particular, sprang from the traditional view of the community college mission: providing open access to higher education. There was fear that such programs would undermine the traditional community college mission (Floyd & Skolnik, 2005), a fear that continues to be shared by some in the Nevada System of Higher Education.

We agree it is wise for community college stakeholders to hold dear the principle of open access to higher education. After all, one of the chief objectives of a community college is to democratize access to higher education. There is now plenty of evidence that the traditional community college mission at Great Basin College maintains considerable strength. In 2007 the author asked a population of what are now considered "comprehensive colleges" questions regarding the effect of bachelor's degree programs on the traditional community college mission. The primary question was, "are enrollments in university transfer courses, developmental courses, and applied career and technical education courses affected when a community college engages in the delivery of a baccalaureate degree?"

An inquiry was made into three areas considered critical to the community college mission: (1) open admission and access to lower-division university transfer courses, (2) developmental instruction, and (3) applied career and technical education or vocational course work. There had been a considerable amount of worry that enrollments in these areas would be affected by the onset of bachelor's degree programs. So, trends in enrollments in the years prior to and post the initiation of those programs were examined. The study identified peer institutions with characteristics defined by another member of the GBC academy, Dr. Danny Gonzalez, in 2005. His work identified peers as those with a Carnegie Classification as an associate college, one publicly governed and regionally accredited, and with the highest degree awarded being the baccalaureate. They are the peer group considered to be engaged in the delivery of the community college baccalaureate.

The study queried 14 peer institutions fitting those criteria. The institutions reported FTE enrollment numbers in lower division university transfer instruction, developmental instruction, and applied career and technical education instruction in the three years prior to and three years post the commencement of the baccalaureate program. Responses varied, but trends were apparent and provided a critical view of the effect of the community college baccalaureate on the traditional community college mission. Furthermore, the aggregate results mirrored the results experienced by Great Basin College.

Overall, the institutions reported what could be termed dramatic net increases in enrollments, with developmental instruction increasing by 95% and lower-division university transfer enrollments increasing by 21%. However, career and technical education (CTE) enrollments decreased by 1% overall. The reports showed that within the peer group respondents, the introduction of the baccalaureate coincided with a positive effect on two characteristics of the traditional community college mission and no significant negative effect on the third.

At Great Basin College, it ought to be noted that regional business and industry required more baccalaureate-prepared employees than career and technical education completers. Thus, the benign downward change in CTE graduates was a result of GBC responding to exactly what the community needed.

Perhaps more telling than the numbers is the narrative that continues to support the development of community college bachelor's degree programs. Leadership was asked questions regarding the effect of bachelor degrees on their traditional missions. When presidents were asked if their institutions had intended to maintain the traditional community college mission, they were unanimous in their strong agreement. The peer institutions intended to maintain their traditional mission, and leadership took steps to ensure that would be the case. Such was certainly the case at Great Basin College. The community college mission remains very strong.

More of the responses suggest that strong leadership will ensure the preservation of the traditional community college mission as baccalaureate programs begin. At Great Basin College, for instance, the choice to appoint a dean to oversee traditional community college programming had a good result.

All of the leaders surveyed agreed their constituents perceive that their institutions have maintained the traditional community college mission. However, the results suggested a certain percentage of their constituency is not as convinced as the leadership. Strategies for showing how the traditional community college mission continues to maintain strength could benefit the institutions. At Great Basin College, when the president and the chief development officer toured the entire service area and held intensive listening sessions with stakeholders in each of the communities it served, subsequent surveys showed stakeholders remain confident in the comprehensive mission of GBC. They know the value of CTE training and its link to employment opportunities in the rural Nevada economy. They also fully understand the importance of the bachelor's degree programs and see its advantage in home-growing professionals, especially in areas where it has historically been difficult to recruit and retain personnel.

When leadership was asked if their faculty members were committed to the traditional community college mission, there was a mixed response. All reported their faculty members were committed to the traditional mission; however, some suggested that select faculty were committed to one and not the other. When GBC began to hire PhDs to teach in its baccalaureate programs, it was noted that some, having come from a university setting, were unprepared for the rigors of a community college workload. In response, the college implemented a successful effort among existing faculty to obtain their doctorate degrees. GBC not only committed to "growing their own" in the bachelor's degree ranks, it grew its own at the doctoral level as well. Encouraging that pursuit was arguably one of the smartest moves the college made. The entire population of peer institutions was aligned with the position of Great Basin College: They were all student-centered learning institutions. Students *learn* at community colleges, and it remains true with a comprehensive college.

It is common knowledge in the academy that community college enrollment numbers can vary considerably in response to local, regional, or national economic conditions. So, presidents were asked whether any unusual economic factors influenced enrollments in associate and university transfer courses, developmental courses, and applied career and technical education courses. Many community college baccalaureate programs came into being while the United States was enjoying the relatively robust economy of the 1990s. Not surprisingly, the area where enrollments were flat in the peer institutions was in CTE course work. Theoretically, students who might seek training in those areas were working, so enrollments would naturally be lower. On the other hand, enrollments in developmental and transfer areas increased dramatically. This was true at Great Basin College. Students who sought credentials beyond the associate's degree took advantage of the new opportunity for democratic access to the bachelor's degree. GBC saw a notable spike in enrollments in bachelor of applied science programs, designed to provide a student with an earned associate's degree a pathway to the baccalaureate. Many trained and experienced technicians in the region's mining industry who had graduated from GBC's CTE programs years earlier returned for the opportunity to advance their positions by earning a BAS.

Advisory boards were extremely important to the success of Great Basin College's sortie into baccalaureate programs. Peer institutions engaged in establishing them as well. It was a key ingredient to developing the program, and a key ingredient to marketing the new idea throughout the service area. GBC's advisory boards were hands on, especially in developing the initial degree programs. Clearly, the establishment of a strong advisory board and the board's commitment to developing and arguing on behalf of the community college baccalaureate was important to its initial success.

Throughout the peer institutions, the advisory boards were split in their commitment to preserving the traditional mission. Approximately 70% of the presidents reported their advisory boards were strongly in favor of preserving the traditional mission. The other 30%, a number perhaps too big to ignore, were nearly as adamant that it not be preserved, though the presidents of those institutions continued to use their own leadership to maintain them. (It could be argued that the significant number of respondents who held little or no commitment to the traditional mission had visions of moving beyond the comprehensive college to something more in line with a state college or university. There are many contemporary and historical examples of that sort of transformation. On the other hand, GBC joins other colleges, such as Brigham Young University–Idaho, with a durable commitment to its unique comprehensive college mission.) Ultimately, the findings suggest that the leadership of a comprehensive college controls the destiny of its mission. It is *commitment* to mission that will *maintain* mission. That commitment has been the key to GBC's continued strength.

Higher education in any of its forms has historically responded to a need in a community. The literature points to scores of examples where community colleges have acted in response to a need in the community. When presidents were asked if their bachelor's degree programs were developed in response to a need in their communities, they all answered "yes." It could not be truer at Great Basin College. Nevada's rapid growth in the 1990s had created a critical shortage of K–12 educators. Rural Nevada communities especially were dependent on recruiting newly minted teachers from Midwestern states. When positions opened in their home states, they returned, often leaving holes in the K–12 faculty ranks. GBC's teacher education program grew its own new teachers. They had grown up in rural Nevada school districts, studied education in a rural Nevada college, and returned to successfully teach a new generation of young rural Nevadans in the schools they grew up in. Pride grew, effectiveness grew, and the reason for implementing the program was confirmed. And, it did not stop at education. Great Basin College had for more than two decades effectively trained technicians in a variety of CTE disciplines who took good jobs in the local mining industry. After 10 or 15 years, those technicians were rising into supervisory positions. However, they didn't have the management skills required to be most effective. So, in response to a call from business and industry, GBC then developed a Bachelor of Applied Science Program in Management Technology. Trained technicians returned to GBC (and, because of flexible scheduling and distance learning technologies, continued to work full time) and acquired the skills and credentials to be effective managers. Again, GBC invested in the professionals required to sustain the regional workforce.

Nearly all of the institutions approached the development of bachelor's degree programs with fitting gravitas. Most engaged in an intensive feasibility study prior to the initiation of the baccalaureate. The exploration of the feasibility of a baccalaureate program provided instruction to an institution in regard to its commitment to the traditional mission. The community summits that Great Basin College engaged in after the programs were established provided additional instruction and prompted another look at how to respond to the needs of business and industry. Great Basin College Foundation, for instance, used the findings of the community summits to determine the focus of a major giving campaign. Because the current Nevada economy begs for sustainability, GBC Foundation will fund programs in emerging technology, which will provide the venture capital the college needs to develop or strengthen programs in emerging technological opportunities, many in renewable energy and health sciences.

Finally, presidents were asked how well the missions of their institutions were understood regarding the provision of both traditional community college programming and the baccalaureate degree. Responses ranged across the spectrum and suggested it was challenging to bring the entire institution on board with the notion. One of the hallmarks of Great Basin College's original plan to develop bachelor's degree programs was a reliance on an integrative curriculum. Because the number of faculty members was small, the idea was that faculty from diverse disciplines (say, science and theater) would create integrative upper-division course work that would fulfill degree requirements and provide students with a diverse education. It was a great idea and had considerable support at the onset.

The concept of an integrative curriculum was to capitalize on four assets immediately available to the college. First was the expertise of the existing faculty. Second, it could provide students with the opportunity to read and discuss primary source material. Third, the college could create a writing-intensive academic experience. Lastly and perhaps most importantly, the college could provide students with the opportunity to learn from a team of expert instructors bringing a broad and diverse background to each upper-division course.

The expertise of the existing faculty was elemental to the idea. GBC had strong faculty members in both applied career and technical and academic disciplines. When a professor in an applied area teamed with a professor in an academic area, the results were dramatic. Both students and instructors became "scholar-practitioners." They were literally able to put their hands on the theories being taught. As an example, a welding and math instructor could team. The result would be, for example, a student with a welding background would learn the formulas that dictate the requirements for a structural weld. Conversely, a student with a mathematics background would learn the skills required to make their mathematical concept a reality. Copernicus meets the Discovery Channel. In the end, the student would be just what the local economy ordered: an employee with the skills to get a job done and the insight to know why it is important. An added bonus: Professors broadened their own body of knowledge. (And both would take those traits into the community as well, enhancing the quality of life for an entire population.)

Sadly, the idea of team teaching has fallen by the wayside, a victim of budget restraints, the loss of veteran faculty members who conceived, implemented, and valued the idea, and a lack of administrative intervention to maintain it. It has also resulted in a return to "department silos," probably the least desirable path for a small college with limited resources (and a challenge the college should address aggressively). A decade ago there was great enthusiasm for teaching and learning across disciplines. Collaboration was viral. It was what set the Great Basin College baccalaureate programs apart from most others. Such is no longer the case, and it is the biggest weakness of the programs today.

Conclusion

So, what does all of this mean? Certainly, the principle of access to higher education provided by the traditional community college is dear. When President Obama convened the White House Summit on Community Colleges, its importance was raised to the executive offices of the nation. It was a significant step in the advancement of democratic access to higher education. One breakout session at the summit focused on the Pathway to the Baccalaureate. In that session there was some discussion of the bachelor of applied science as an opportunity for technically skilled persons with an earned associate of applied science degree to advance their own positions. However, there was no discussion of the comprehensive baccalaureate offerings provided by an institution like Great Basin College, where critical community needs are filled by the presence of bachelor's programs. So, the journey of the comprehensive college must continue.

This chapter discusses the Community Summits the GBC Foundation engaged in. It became a terrific opportunity for feedback on the effectiveness of the comprehensive approach GBC has taken to higher education. Overwhelming support for GBC's comprehensive mission was documented in each community the college serves. The information provides more evidence of the strength of the comprehensive college model, especially at the grassroots level.

Democratic access to higher education is most important not at the level of academic discussion, but on the ground in the communities where those opportunities are actually making a difference.

Here is why. In each community served by GBC, two critical needs were expressed: First, a concern that shortages of technically skilled employees would occur in the short term (the next eighteen months) and the long term (three to five years). Second, they spoke of the difficulty of recruiting and then retaining professionals in education and health care, as well as professional areas not served by the baccalaureate programs. Both technically and professionally prepared employees are critical to the economic sustainability of rural Nevada. Both are addressed by the comprehensive mission of Great Basin College. In order to serve rural Nevada properly, GBC must have a strong comprehensive mission, and research shows it can effectively and efficiently maintain such a mission.

However, GBC faces challenges. The state of Nevada has wrestled with a bust in its economy since 2008. While the rest of the nation begins to recover, Nevada lags behind because of its reliance on gaming and growth for its revenues. It used to be that a college like GBC was asked to do more with less. Now, it seems, the college is being asked to simply do less with much less. The formula puts the sustainability of its strong comprehensive achievements in jeopardy.

The challenges are not only fiscal. The Complete College America (CCA) program, with its emphasis on raising completion rates for students earning a "credential of value" has administrators scrambling to recognize even the smallest of academic achievements to fulfill its terms. It is much easier to run a student through a certificate program than it is for the student to complete a bachelor's degree. There is appreciation for the opportunities and support provided by CCA. However, it's not what China is doing. In order for our nation to be innovative and competitive, we must produce not only skilled applied technologists, we must produce skilled professionals. And, we must produce them everywhere.

At a 2010 United States Senate Rural Steering Committee meeting, Senate leaders underscored the importance of rural communities in the recovery and sustainability of the nation's economy. More and more small manufacturing and service organizations are moving their operations to communities the size of those served by Great Basin College. The reason: the small town values and work ethic. Business and industry know that employees in smaller communities tend to know how to work well. They also want the professionals in their organizations to have a personal relationship with their employees. Their kids go to school together, they see each other's families in church, and they go to ball games and picnics. Small-town values; big-time economic return.

That is why the community college bachelor's degree programs at Great Basin College are so important. It is one of "the peoples colleges" (Floyd & Skolnik, 2005), with its roots deeply set in strong, student-centered success. GBC's programs have been responsive to the evolutionary needs of its rural communities. It has consistently shown strength and rigor. Its transformation has been metamorphic, with its traditional community college mission now the mission of the 21st Century Comprehensive College. Great Basin College provides individuals, entire communities, and indeed the nation, continued access to the fulfillment of the American Dream.

References

Floyd, D. L., & Skolnik, M. L. (2005). Perspectives on the baccalaureate. In D. L. Floyd, M. L. Skolnik, & K. P. Walker (Eds.), *The community college baccalaureate: Emerging trends and policies* (pp. 1–8). Sterling, VA: Stylus.

Gonzales, D. A. (2004). *Identifying peer institutions: Creating a utilized focused analysis of community colleges conferring select baccalaureate degrees* (Doctoral dissertation, University of Nevada, Reno). Available from ProQuest Dissertations and Theses Database.

Rice, J. P. (2010). *Proceedings from White House Summit on Community Colleges, 2010*. Washington, DC.

Rice, J. P. (2010). *Proceedings from United States Senate Rural Caucus, 2010*. Washington, DC.

Rice, J. P. (2007). *Mission Metamorphosis: How Community College Bachelor Degree Programs Influence the Traditional Community College Mission* (Doctoral dissertation, Capella University, Minneapolis, MN). Available from ProQuest Dissertations and Theses Database.

Rothman, J., & Friedman, V. J. (2004). *Action Evaluation: Helping to Define, Assess, and Achieve Organizational Goals*. The Action Evaluation Research Institute. Retrieved from http://www.aepro.org/inprint/papers/aedayton.html

4

STUDENT VOICES

The Impact of Access on Individual Lives

Edith Pendleton

In this chapter, college students from the United States and Canada describe the impact of the community college baccalaureate on their educations, their careers, and their lives. Their narratives describe the socioeconomic consequences of a college education for themselves and their families, as well as for their communities, offering firsthand accounts of the journey toward upward mobility and a better future. Etched in hope, their experiences record academic careers of courage and determination.

Clarence Ranow of Fort Myers, Florida, put the life of the community college student in perspective when he said, "We don't have fraternities and sororities, we have families. We don't have dorms, we have mortgages. Extracurricular activities? We call those jobs. We are rooted in the community, unable to transfer to another college" (1999).

A study of higher-education challenges, authored by the American Association of Community Colleges, in conjunction with the American Association of State Colleges and Universities, reveals that "the credibility and effectiveness of the American higher education system—long the strength of our democracy and a model for the world—are on the line. Unique to the nature of that system is the implicit promise that educational opportunity and the better quality of life it brings are open to all. Universal access, then, becomes both our standard and our pledge" (2004, p. viii).

Yet thousands of students who aspire to baccalaureate attainment cannot afford escalating tuition and the multiple ancillary expenses that encompass the price of a college degree. Nor can they ignore their competing life obligations—family, community, employment—that require them to be close to home. In addition to financial and competing commitments, students face barriers of language and degree status. The question then is can we afford to exclude these 21st century students from an education necessary for individual and family dignity, satisfying work, and engaged citizenry?

According to a 2002 study compiled by the Advisory Committee on Student Financial Assistance for Congress, "Financial barriers prevent 48% of college-qualified, low-income high school graduates from attending a four-year college and 22% from attending any college at all, within two years of graduation." It goes on to say that, "for middle-income families, 43% are unable to attend a 4-year college and 16% attend no college at all" (p. v).

The report concluded that "the nation will have to increase the enrollment and degree completion rates of low-and-moderate income students or bring in highly skilled foreign workers to meet the demand," (Advisory Committee on Student Financial Assistance, p. 3) adding that "the vibrancy of our democracy and our knowledge-based economy is dependent upon ensuring access to college for these students" (p. 4).

In 2011, it seems these projections have become a reality. College costs have increased by 50% over the last decade, while family incomes have actually fallen. When young adults were asked recently, by a Pew Research Center/*Chronicle* survey, why they're not enrolled in college or don't have a bachelor's degree, their response was: money (Fischer, 2011).

In an article published in *The Community College Review*, authors Richard W. Zinser and Carl. E. Hanssen (2006) note that in addition to prohibitive costs, another issue is emerging. "Increasingly worrisome is the significant shift from need-based to merit-based financial aid in many states, making it more difficult for low-income students to qualify for the financial assistance they need in order to cover the spiraling costs of student tuition and fees" (p. 7).

As a result of cost increases, the percentage of people who believe that a college education "is out of reach for many qualified students" has risen over the last decade, up from 47% in 2000 to 69% in 2009 (Immerwahr & Johnson, 2010, p. 3).

In researching his options, Matthew S. Long of Cape Fear Community College in Wilmington, North Carolina, found that the average price that in-state students pay for baccalaureate degrees at conferring colleges and universities is $30,420. Attending private colleges *more than triples* the price of public college education, with an average total cost of more than $105,092, he found. "The credit crisis of 2007–2010 taught the United States the foolishness of abusing unlimited credit, and should not be forgotten. The 'buy now, pay later' concept (which is a rampant problem among students) should be eradicated among individuals pursuing higher education" (personal communication, May 7, 2012).

The following passages include the personal accounts of four other students. Student Jodi-Lynn Terracina of Ocala, Florida, concurs with Long's assessment:

> When I began researching baccalaureate degree programs, the cost of tuition at the universities was prohibitive. I thought my road ended with my associate degree. Then I realized the College of Central Florida would begin offering baccalaureate degrees in 2011! It was like winning the lottery! The cost of tuition is significantly lower than tuition at a University, and I can stay at the school that I love. My community college experience thus far has been extremely positive; having wonderful professors with small class sizes. Earning my associate degree at CFCC left me with knowledge that opened doors of opportunity and opened my eyes to a new world. (personal communication, November 3, 2002)

Mounting expenses associated with university life nearly crushed his college aspirations, Jeremy Hayden of Barrie, Ontario, says.

> With the cost of post-secondary education increasing, it would have been near impossible to go back to school if my four-year degree was not offered through my community college. If I were required to attend a post-secondary institution outside of my community I would have to obtain transportation, a new vehicle, to commute to and from home or incur the cost of a second residence. (personal communication, November 3, 2010)

Actor Matthew Keeslar of Portland, Oregon, describes his experiences as a young father suddenly faced with inadequate credentials for a career change.

> Last May I realized that we would run out of money in ten weeks. I had been struggling as an actor in Los Angeles while my wife taught piano lessons. My son was about to start preschool. Although I happened upon success earlier in my career, I hadn't worked in over a year. We had stretched our budget to its limit. My wife and I cobbled together a plan: We would sell our house and bunk up with my in-laws while I churned through the prerequisites for nursing school.
>
> I enrolled at Portland State, but because my parents-in-law lived in Oregon and we were coming from California, I was considered a non-resident. The tuition floored me. I would have to borrow huge loans. If I

were not accepted into nursing school, I would have to find a job and start repaying those loans immediately. I ditched that plan and enrolled at Portland Community College.

The safety net of community college caught me before I hit bottom. Without the low cost and guaranteed admission I would have had to take a minimum-wage job to support my family. Portland Community College offered me the opportunity to improve my academic record and work toward a Bachelor's of Science in Nursing. As hospitals strive to fill positions with the best candidates, and nurses take on an increasingly important role in health care, the BSN has become a crucial element in securing a job after graduation. Enrolling in a community college is giving me the chance to enter the work force with the training I need to succeed. (personal communication, February 7, 2011)

Timothy R. Grubbs of Santa Fe College in Gainesville, Florida, agrees:

It may seem a stretch comparing community colleges to Hollywood-style freedom fighters, but for many of us struggling to climb out of the cycle of poverty, the organizations we call community colleges are true heroes. They appear in the right place, at the right time, and help people overcome dire situations, and my case is no different. Growing up, our family was dirt poor. My father worked relentlessly at the jobs he could get, but he only had an eighth grade education. My mother faced battles with addictions, and our family suffered the consequences. All along, I dreamed of moving beyond that world, to a place where people live well and do important things. Right after graduation, I landed a good job in the IT industry, we bought our first house, and the road ahead looked bright. That was, until the economy crashed three years ago, and I became a casualty of downsizing. I hunted for jobs and tried self-employment with limited success, as people and businesses drew back on their purse strings. Shortly, I found myself out of money and options, with a family and bills to pay. I looked back at Santa Fe, and they were offering four-year degrees. I started the process, was approved for financial aid, and am now on track to earn a Baccalaureate degree with honors. I am continuing to move forward, and breaking the cycle for our daughter, but none of this would have been possible without Santa Fe. By providing affordable tuition, flexible schedules, distance learning, and partnering with universities to offer baccalaureate programs, students like me are given a foot in the door to opportunities that would otherwise be unreachable. I am living proof that community colleges create hope and opportunity every day for people who desperately need both. (personal communication, November 26, 2011)

Dramatic demographic shifts have profoundly impacted community college populations. A summary of its March 2008 report, "Knocking at the College Door: Projections of High School Graduates by State and Race/ Ethnicity 1992–2022," Western Interstate Commission for Higher Education (WICHE) reports, "Our nation and many states will also witness a dramatic shift in the racial/ethnic composition of their student bodies and high school graduating classes, with rising numbers of graduates from populations our educational institutions haven't served well in the past—especially Hispanics— offsetting a substantial decline in white non-Hispanic graduates" (Longanecker, 2008).

According to Demaree Michelau, WICHE's director of policy analysis, key barriers preventing students from completing a college degree include:

Competing "life" obligations.
Lack of familiarity with recent changes in campus processes.
Financial holds on registration.

"Most stop-outs left because life happened, not because they were failing out or doing badly," Michelau notes. "If you make it to your senior year, you are probably doing okay. These students left because there was a death in the family, or because they were deployed, or their spouses were deployed. Something big happened. They didn't just reach the second semester of their senior year and suddenly decide this degree wasn't for them. . . . Higher education is now competing with commitments that are arguably as important if not more important in their lives" (Fusch, 2010)

Consider Domenic Caloia, for example.

When the economy nosedived two years ago I lost more than my job, I lost hope. At a time when friends were planning for retirement, I was refinancing my home and desperately looking for a job. I was heartbroken to discover that decades of work experience took a back seat to a four-year college degree, a requirement that I did not have.

[Upon enrolling in St. Petersburg College, he discovered that] new ideas stretched my imagination and challenged my thinking. The encouragement I received from professors and students alike helped me to believe in myself at a time when the world was slamming doors on me. Working together with other students, my communication skills improved as we learned from each other. I gradually realized that I had good ideas worth sharing. The benefits of attaining a bachelor's degree from my community college are not limited to increased employment opportunities alone.

Returning to school may have begun as a desperate necessity, but it quickly became a personal pilgrimage of growth and self-discovery. Inspired with a newfound confidence and an optimistic outlook, I am planning to continue my studies in graduate school. (personal communication, February 7, 2011)

In *The Missing Class: Portraits of the Near Poor in America*, Katherine Newman and Victor Tan Chen examine the barriers to education that afflict 57 million poor Americans "who constitute a fifth of our population" (2007, p. 225). Their case-based study revealed that it takes years "for adults in this class to complete their education, in part because our financial-aid system was never designed to support the kind of intermittent learning that fits their schedules and needs" (p. B10).

In 2007, Paul Attewell and David E. Lavin published the results of a study that refutes established perceptions about the scholastic potential of minority and underrepresented college freshmen. Tracking the City College of New York's class of 1970, the researchers discovered that "29 percent of women completed their degrees over ten years after they first entered college, and 10 percent completed them twenty or more years after entry. The low graduation rates that scandalize critics of public higher education are typically measured only four or six years after entry to college. When one takes a longer view, a much more positive picture emerges" (p. 5). Their findings describe the challenges of underrepresented students, who rarely enjoy the luxury of four years on a university campus far from the demands of everyday life.

Student Neira D. Rodriquez of Hidalgo, Texas, says South Texas College offered "affordable education on a silver tray." She writes:

I am a Mexican-American who longs for success. Earning a four-year degree means a better job and consequently, a better standard of living that we, as a migrant family have worked too hard to obtain. STC offers me quality and applied education for much less than a university would cost, an education that gets me the same level of job close to home. As a Mexican American, I am very family attached; this is part of my culture. It is for this reason I could not endure being at a university far from home. (personal communication, November 3, 2009)

Adds Maryknoll Palisoc, a College of Southern Nevada student:

Coming from a low-income immigrant family, I did not have the means to directly attend a university. Moreover, as the eldest of four sisters, I wanted to help my parents in providing for the family. I decided to work while attending a community college near our home. The college offered me more than accessibility to my classes. It gave me hope to pursue my dreams. I cannot imagine myself being a fulltime student while working part time if I have gone directly to a four-year school. I was able to pay for my classes while still having the money to help my parents and sisters. (personal communication, November 3, 2010)

According to Attewell and Lavin (2008), a third of college students work full time, and another 44% work part time. In assessing their college experience, these work-savvy students measure results in the context of career advancement, as Krystal Kinley of Grafton, Ohio, explains.

Due to their own particular circumstances, almost all of my classmates will continue to reside and seek employment in Lorain County, where the community college is located. Due to this composition, I have been able to build a professional network with my graduating cohort that I can use in my future profession. (personal communication, November 3, 2010)

Seasoned workforce training collaborators, community college administrators have historically cultivated clinical partners in developing fields. Zach Kilburn, a Canadian student, attends New Brunswick Community College, where he is completing a baccalaureate degree.

In my chosen field of Nuclear Medicine Technology I will require a degree to work in my field in Canada. Rather than seek a degree at a nearby university, I chose the community college because of its superior hands-on experience.

A task force convened by the Higher Learning Commission (2000) to analyze the merits of baccalaureate degrees conferred by community colleges drew the following conclusions:

Possession of a baccalaureate degree is becoming fundamental to career access and career mobility.

Baccalaureate education should fulfill public needs . . . ensuring U.S. preeminence in a global economy.

Baccalaureate providers will need to balance the values of the academy with changing needs of students and the communities in which they live and work.

> Competition is driving responsiveness by baccalaureate institutions, resulting
> in their mounting . . . new applied baccalaureate programs even as they
> explore creative articulation efforts with two year institutions. (p. 4)

The technical and applied baccalaureate degrees employers seek are often
unavailable at state universities, in such fields as public safety management
and radiographic technology.

Community colleges, on the other hand, have the flexibility and workforce savvy to respond quickly and effectively to change, collaborate with
sister institutions, and develop innovative programs on a shoestring, Steven
Graeter of Nashville, Tennessee, argues:

> Our nation's workforce faces stiff competition from international sources
> unimagined a generation ago. Thus if community colleges are to produce
> graduates who will compete in the emerging global marketplace, tradi-
> tional paradigms cannot be sustained. Working adults have a tremendous
> stake in the success of local economies. These non-traditional students face
> a dilemma—requiring additional education beyond a two year degree but
> unable to leave their communities to attain it. (personal communication,
> November 3, 2006)

Student Charles Williams of Pellissippi State Community College in
Lenoir City, Tennessee, puts his views this way:

> For years community colleges have been thought of as places where sub-
> par students who cannot get into a major university go to get remedial
> training, or who simply cannot afford to attend a large school. This is no
> longer true. America's community colleges are places of excellence that
> compare favorably with the four-year schools. Most community colleges
> have a keen sense of the needs of the community and surrounding region,
> and by offering 2 + 2 programs with four-year colleges they help students
> to attend locally and stay in the community. Attending school in a 2 + 2
> program helps communities to keep their very best and brightest members
> locally, and this only strengthens the area by providing an educated work-
> force that also is a part of the very fabric and lifeblood of the community
> the school serves. . . . This is why I am pursuing a 2 + 2 program at Pellis-
> sippi State Community College. Not only will I have a degree in a field
> that will help our national economy and the environment, I will be giving
> back to the community I love so much.

The mission of the community college has changed, as have its students,
Naomi L. Brown of St. Philips Community College in San Antonio, Texas,
says:

Many academics believe that changing the mission of the community college will be devastating. However, I see a new mission, one that will assist students who may not be able to afford or find a baccalaureate degree. . . . A mission that opens the doors in high need careers. I am a 46-year-old African American woman returning to college, a student who earned 104 credits at a university in another state 25 years ago. I started at St. Philips taking two classes. Two years later I've been inducted into Phi Theta Kappa honor society and I am a member of the Student Leadership Institute. To get the bachelor's degree I desire in San Antonio, Texas, I must now transfer to a private university, ten times the cost of my community college. Reluctantly, I leave the nurturing, affordable environment of the community college and return to the university system. (personal communication, November 3, 2006)

"Historically community colleges have fought for an identity, and after 100 years, we're still fighting for respect," according to Kenneth P. Walker, founder of the Community College Baccalaureate Association. "Our students know the quality is there, but they also experience the stigma of attending a community college, and the assumption that you couldn't quite cut it at a university. The change helps dispel the stigma and instill pride in the students and their achievements. That's important because it generates confidence. It makes the students feel like first-class rather than second-class citizens" (personal communication, August 13, 2010).

Edison State College student Zuly Fernandez, a Cuban refugee, concurs.

It is imperative for me to earn a baccalaureate degree while living at home because my family cannot afford the expense of dormitory housing. Furthermore, I can continue to work and contribute to household expenses. Originally, community colleges were designed to assist students like me, who came through the door already burdened with financial need, language barriers and family adversity that made admission to a university inconceivable. I am among thousands of students who not only succeeded in the supportive environment of the community college, but far exceeded their wildest dreams, and consequently aspire to a baccalaureate. (personal communication, November 3, 2005)

In *The Post-American World*, best-selling author Fareed Zakaria contends that America's edge in innovation results from its influx of immigrants. "Foreign students and immigrants account for 50 percent of the science researchers in the country, and in 2006 received 40 percent of the doctorates in science and engineering and 65 percent of the doctorates in computer science" (2008, p. 198).

If we intend to solve the problems of public education, we must encourage the initiative and efficiency that spring from creative thinking. If legislators expect to improve performance, enhance productivity, and save money, they must ignite the entrepreneurial vigor of educators, encouraging the development of market-driven, market-tested, individualized enterprises that nurture learning and inspire students to stay the course.

References

Advisory Committee on Student Financial Assistance. (2002, June). *Empty promises: The myth of college access in America* (Report). Washington, DC: Author. Retrieved from http://www2.ed.gov/about/bdscomm/list/acsfa/emptypromises.pdf

American Association of Community Colleges and American Association of State Colleges and Universities. (2004). *Improving access to the baccalaureate.* Washington, DC: Community College Press.

Attewell, P., & Lavin, D. (2007). *Passing the torch: Does higher education for the disadvantaged pay off across the generations?* New York, NY: Russell Sage Foundation.

Attewell, P., & Lavin, D. (2008). *The other 75%: College education beyond the elite.* Remarks made at Weinberg Seminar. April 15. Data are from the Beginning postsecondary students longitudinal study, American Association of Community Colleges, 2004.

Fischer, K. (2011). Crisis of confidence threatens colleges. *The Chronicle of Higher Education.* Retrieved from http://chronicle.com/article/A-Crisis-of-Confidence/127530/

Fusch, D. (2010). *Re-enrolling stop-outs: Overcoming the barriers.* Academic Impressions, July 15, 2010. Retrieved from http://www.academicimpressions.com/news.php?i=94&q=5952v274891vT

Higher Learning Commission. (2000). *Baccalaureate education in the community college setting executive summary.* Tempe, AZ: North Central Association of Colleges and Schools.

Immerwahr, J., & Johnson, J. (2010). *Squeeze play 2010: Continued public anxiety on cost, harsher judgments on how colleges are run.* Washington, DC: National Center for Public Policy and Higher Education and Public Agenda.

Longanecker, D. (2008). Foreword. *Knocking at the college door: Projections of high school graduate by state and race/ethnicity 1992–2022* (p. xi). Boulder, CO: Western Interstate Commission for Higher Education (WICHE). Retrieved from http://www.wiche.edu/info/publications/knocking_complete_book.pdf

Newman, K. S., & Tan Chen, V. (2005, October 5). The crisis of the near poor. *The Chronicle Review, 54*(6), B10.

Newman, K. S., & Tan Chen, V. (2007). *The missing class: Portraits of the near poor in America.* Boston, MA: Beacon Press.

Ranow, C. (1999, March). Remarks made to the Edison State College District Board of Trustees.

Zakaria, F. (2008). *The post American world.* New York, NY: Norton.

Zinser, R. W., & Hanssen, C. E. (2006). Improving access to the baccalaureate: Articulation agreements and national science foundation advanced technological education program. *Community College Review, 34*(1), 7.

5

IMPACT ON ACCREDITATION STATUS WHEN COMMUNITY COLLEGES OFFER BACCALAUREATE DEGREES

Belle S. Wheelan and Tom Benberg

For well over 100 years, assessing the quality of an institution and its curricular offerings has been the responsibility of the regional accrediting agencies. This peer review process has ensured that institutions of higher education are indeed offering programs and services appropriate for postsecondary learning. One of the hallmarks of our system of higher education has been the diversity of institutional types, curricular offerings, and pedagogical approaches available for students. Examples include public or private governance models; diploma, certificate, associates, and baccalaureate degree curricular structures; and face-to-face, online, or blended pedagogical approaches. Regardless of the type of institution, curriculum, or pedagogical approach, all are expected to meet established guidelines to ensure the quality of student learning.

When community colleges began, one of the initial purposes was to strengthen students' basic skills in order to prepare them for enrollment at universities. The mission of these "junior colleges" was expanded when the GI Bill made it possible for military personnel returning from the war to bring their military training to the classroom and convert it into academic credits through occupational programs. Because many of these institutions were funded by local communities, community service programming was added as part of the official mission of the community's college. Additionally, in order to meet the needs of the residents of the community, these institutions maintained an open door policy, making it possible for all to attend college in order to make a better life for themselves. Because many residents did not have the skill sets needed to successfully complete college level work, these institutions began to offer remediation.

Over time, the four focal areas of transfer, occupational training, community service, and remediation have become the major components of the mission of community colleges. In addition, most community colleges have maintained open door admission policies accompanied by low tuition. These concepts and attendant best practices have often been emulated by many nations around the world. It is this mission and its components that have been used to assess the quality of community colleges through the accreditation process; however, for those community colleges currently offering baccalaureate degrees, the mission has been expanded again. What impact(s) does this then have on the accreditation of these institutions? This chapter will attempt to answer that question.

Mission

The decision by some community colleges to offer baccalaureate degree programs has brought into question whether the addition of these programs has changed the mission significantly enough to affect the accreditation status of the institution and trigger a qualitative review. Standards established by each of the regional accrediting bodies and reinforced by the rules and regulations of the U.S. Department of Education require every institution that makes substantive changes to notify the accreditation agency of the anticipated change(s) and, in many cases, secure advance approval and subsequently host an evaluation committee. The purpose for this process is to ensure that the programs, services, and resources are appropriate for the level of degree programming offered.

Currently, the majority of the baccalaureate degrees offered at community colleges are in areas that are not offered at neighboring senior institutions, or that assist in meeting employment demands within the local community. However, once an associate's degree granting institution receives approval to offer specific degree programming at the baccalaureate level, it opens the door for the possibility of offering additional programs that fall outside of those two parameters. This is sometimes called the beginning of "mission creep."

Selection of an appropriate substantive change evaluation committee is a challenge when an institution expands to offer baccalaureate degrees.

Although the baccalaureate degree level programming clearly must be reviewed, many times much of the associate's degree level programming must also be reviewed to determine its applicability to a coherent baccalaureate degree. Thus, decisions must be made about how to best constitute evaluation committee membership. Should the members come from only baccalaureate granting institutions or should there be a mixture of reviewers from both associate and baccalaureate institutions? This decision is driven largely by the nature of the mission change and the structure of programming that follows.

Faculty Qualifications

Having a core teaching faculty who are well qualified in their respective fields is at the heart of any institution of higher education—no matter the mission and level of degrees, certificates, or diplomas offered. Most educators believe that lower-division courses intended for transfer or inclusion in a baccalaureate degree should include higher-level thinking skills and be taught by faculty with higher qualifications than courses intended for immediate employment readiness. This could create some controversy in the accreditation process. However, whether in the general education core or in specific academic areas, faculty must demonstrate that they have the skills necessary to effectively teach the content of the courses and programs they offer and ensure that the appropriate level of student learning is achieved. These skills are generally acquired through the successful completion of academic programs resulting in the awarding of degrees; however, there are other ways that faculty can demonstrate their competence to teach. Examples include professional licensure and certifications, honors, and awards. It is the responsibility of the institution to document and justify the qualifications of its faculty to any evaluation team.

When community colleges offer baccalaureate degrees, they change the mix of academic programs and, therefore, impact the qualifications needed by the faculty. More advanced preparation is required of those who offer the new "upper-division" courses needed to complete the baccalaureate programs. Faculty who have been teaching "lower-division" courses that make up associate's degree programs might not be qualified to teach in the new degree programs; additionally, faculty who have been teaching lower-division courses not intended for transfer might need additional qualifications if and when those courses become subject to transfer. As a result, institutions might have to engage in aggressive faculty development programs or employ more highly qualified faculty in order to demonstrate compliance with accrediting standards.

Additionally, accrediting bodies generally have established standards that require that a certain proportion of the discipline course hours in each major field of study be taught by faculty members holding the terminal degree, usually the earned doctorate, in the discipline. As the number of course hours increases, because of the addition of upper-division courses, the number of faculty with the terminal degree will also increase as a proportion of the overall teaching faculty.

The bottom line is that both institutions and regional accreditors must wrestle with determining appropriate faculty qualifications.

Curricular Issues

Two of the most important curricular issues, when community colleges offer baccalaureate degrees, are general education and transfer of credits.

The general education component for a baccalaureate degree normally consists of about 30 semester hours taken from each of the following three areas: humanities/fine arts, social/behavioral sciences, and natural sciences/mathematics. For the associate's degree, the general education component usually consists of about 15 semester hours. It is intended that these courses will not narrowly focus on those skills, techniques, and procedures specific to a particular occupation or profession. The general education core is designed to ensure that each student has developed a common, broad foundation of knowledge. However, sometimes in lower division non-transfer programs, the general education courses border on being too specific in their focus. When institutions subsequently incorporate such courses into the general education core for the baccalaureate degree, evaluation committees raise questions.

Determining the appropriateness of lower-division courses/credits subject to transfer and incorporation into the baccalaureate degree is very challenging for both institutions and evaluation committees. One of the challenges occurs when the original purpose of the course is changed so that it can be included in the transfer program, for example, courses not intended for transfer and certificate and diploma courses not intended for inclusion in a degree. A second challenge occurs when courses are not designated by the institution as transfer or non-transfer, thus leaving both students and accreditors to figure this out. A third challenge occurs when the overall degree curriculum is evaluated for coherency and integrity, thus ensuring that the degree is much more than an accumulation of courses. Finally, sometimes course titles and degree names have been shaped to address perceived marketing needs, and they do not accurately reflect the underlying content. Evaluation committees must sort through these and additional curricular issues as they focus on the quality of education students receive. To the extent that institutions are proactive and clarify these matters in their catalogs, and to the extent that institutions have a well-defined, embedded transfer review process, they might reduce confusion and enhance the quality of the evaluation committee's review.

Support Services

Additional emphasis on library and other learning resources and on student and academic support services are typically required when an associate's degree granting institution begins to offer baccalaureate degree programming. Adequate library and other learning resources that specifically align with the new courses/programs should be made available to faculty and students. Student and academic support services that directly address the needs of the new upper-division students must be provided. Accreditors require that institutions provide appropriate support services for their upper-division programming, which could demand employing or training additional personnel.

Planning, Budgeting, and Resources

As new upper-division programs are anticipated, the planning and budgeting functions become very important as the institution considers nonrecurring start up costs as well as recurring operational costs. Sustaining quality without diminishing existing programming is essential.

The central focus in the planning and budgeting process includes considerations of physical facilities, personnel, instruction, support services, and numbers of students. Institutions should conduct needs assessments and benchmark studies in an effort to satisfy the needs of upper-division programming. Additionally, institution leadership should be mindful that accreditors require each institution to provide healthy, safe, and secure environments for the campus community. Again, a demonstration of compliance with this mandate is required.

Fiscally, increased costs for salaries and benefits, library resources, computers and learning laboratory equipment, and utilities are but a few of the areas that are impacted by the addition of new programs. Accreditors require that institutions have sufficient resources to fulfill their mission.

There is no doubt that access to higher educational opportunity is a hallmark of community colleges and, if senior institutions are not able or willing to provide degree programs, then community colleges should step up and do so. Unfortunately, the phrase, "no good deed goes unpunished" is often heard when this occurs. The community college baccalaureate is raising questions in many different arenas. Ultimately, the single overriding question must always be, "What is in the best interest of the students?"

6

UPDATE ON THE COMMUNITY COLLEGE BACCALAUREATE

Evolving Trends and Issues

Alene Bycer Russell

O ver the past two decades, the number of community colleges independently offering baccalaureate degree programs has steadily risen. Though still confined to a very small number of institutions and limited degree programs, this phenomenon continues to generate widespread attention and controversy. This occurs because the trend challenges fundamental assumptions about the mission of two-year colleges and threatens to upset the existing balance between the two- and four-year sectors in the U.S. higher-education system.

To place this development in context, there are several more common policy approaches that involve community colleges in baccalaureate degree production. Such methods—which this chapter intentionally does not focus on—typically involve collaboration between the two- and four-year sectors, where the four-year institution (not the community college) confers the baccalaureate degree. First, many states, systems, and collaborating institutions have developed transfer and articulation agreements, 2 + 2 arrangements, and other cooperative means to facilitate baccalaureate attainment by students who complete their general education requirements at community colleges. A second approach is partnerships between two- and four-year institutions

---

This chapter is based on an earlier publication: Russell, A. (2010, October). "Update on the community college baccalaureate: Evolving trends and issues." *Policy Matters: A Higher Education Policy Brief.* Washington, DC: American Association of State Colleges and Universities.

that bring four-year degree programs on-site to community colleges and other convenient locations where university access is limited—university centers, shared facilities, joint programs, and other arrangements. Finally, online degree programs, enhanced by partnership and transfer agreements, are increasingly available to community college students who seek a bachelor's degree without leaving home. All of these policy options are well established and less controversial. They are continuing to expand nationwide, even in states that have begun to approve independent community college baccalaureate programs.

The focus of our attention is on a specific phenomenon that has arisen largely in response to increased demands for baccalaureate degrees in particular geographic areas and fields of study—often rural locations and high-demand fields, such as education, nursing, and technical subjects. It generally occurs where there is limited access to a four-year institution or where demand exceeds the existing capacity of the four-year sector. This phenomenon is also fueled by the upgraded educational credentials now needed for certain applied and technical fields, occupations in which associate's degrees once sufficed, but where employers now prefer or require workers to possess a four-year degree.

The independently offered community college baccalaureate has virtually never been the first response to meeting these needs. Generally, the community college baccalaureate requires legislative approval, or, at minimum, the approval of a systemwide governing body. Normally, there is a thorough review process through which workforce and student demand must be documented, alternatives explored and exhausted, costs estimated, and community college capacity determined. Following approval, two-year institutions must undergo regional accreditation in order to offer a four-year degree program. Faculty must then be hired, libraries and facilities brought up to speed, and so on. In sum, it is not a trivial endeavor, nor one that can be carried out quickly.

But times are changing, and it is unclear whether past trends will predict the future. The Obama administration has called for the nation to have the highest proportion of college graduates in the world by 2020, despite the tremendous challenges of access, cost, and capacity. As new ideas to meet this goal are being examined, this is a good time to take stock of what is happening with the community college baccalaureate. This chapter presents recent trends in the community college baccalaureate, describes variations among the states and pending issues, summarizes arguments for and against the community college baccalaureate, and presents implications for policy makers considering this option.

Steady Growth of the Community College Baccalaureate

The number of states that have approved at least one community college to offer a baccalaureate program has grown steadily over the past decade, as have the numbers of institutions and degree programs approved. Currently, there are 18 states in which a community college has been approved to offer four-year degrees, compared with 11 states in 2004 (Russell, 2004). There are now 57 institutions that have received such approval, compared with 21 institutions 7 years ago. These institutions now offer—or have been approved to offer—a total of 468 four-year degree programs, compared with 128 programs in 2004. Taken together, these data illustrate the considerable growth in the community college baccalaureate that has taken place in less than a decade (table 6.1).

As part of this trend, there has been substantial growth in baccalaureate-level teacher education programs available at community colleges. Today, 10 states have approved a total of 27 community colleges to offer at least one

TABLE 6.1
Summary of Approved Community College Baccalaureate Programs by State

State	Year of First Approval	Number of Approved Institutions	Total # of Approved Programs	# Offering Teacher Education Programs	# Offering Nursing (BSN) Programs
Arkansas	1998	1	1	1	44
Colorado	2010	1	0	0	0
Florida	2001	18	12	11	113
Georgia	1997	7	6	3	71
Hawaii	2004	1	0	0	2
Indiana	2004	1	1	1	6
Louisiana	2001	1	1	1	12
Minnesota	2003	1	1	0	2
Nevada	1998	3	1	1	15
New Mexico	2004	1	1	1	11
New York	1996	5	0	3	84
North Dakota	2006	1	0	0	1
Oklahoma	2004	2	0	0	4
Texas	2003	3	0	0	4
Utah	1992	2	2	2	69
Vermont	1993	1	0	0	11
Washington	2005	7	0	1	8
West Virginia	1989	1	1	0	11
Total		57	27	25	468

such program. In 2004, 6 states had approved just 9 two-year institutions to offer a baccalaureate in this field. This growth has been stimulated by teacher shortages in specific geographic locations.

Similarly, there has been parallel growth in baccalaureate-level nursing programs available at community colleges. Today, 10 states have approved a total of 25 institutions to offer a bachelor of science in nursing (BSN) at a community college. In 2004, 5 states had approved only 6 community colleges to offer such a program. This tremendous growth is a result of both nursing shortages as well as efforts by the nursing profession to create a more highly educated nursing workforce (i.e., upgrading from the RN to BSN degree).

Identifying and counting these institutions is not an exact science, however, and these totals could be a conservative estimate of this phenomenon. In cases where institutions underwent transformation into baccalaureate institutions some years ago, it was not possible to include them in the count. This accounting is generally consistent with the literature on this topic, which has tracked observable developments since the late 1990s.

As the most recent example of this trend, the Colorado legislature authorized its first community college baccalaureate in 2010. Recognizing the priority of improving access to higher education for citizens in rural areas of the state, Senate Bill (SB) 10-101 authorized Colorado Mountain College, a comprehensive community college with seven physical campuses and distance learning, to offer no more than five baccalaureate degree programs, to be approved by the Colorado Commission on Higher Education. The college must first demonstrate workforce and student demand, comply with all accreditation requirements, demonstrate that its provision of the program "is the most cost-effective method of providing the baccalaureate degree program in the service area," and that the additional program "will not create a negative impact for the college or require additional state appropriated moneys to operate." Surveys to date have shown high demand for programs in resort-related business, teacher education, and environmental science.

Continued Controversy and Opposition

Despite substantial growth, the community college baccalaureate remains a very limited phenomenon, and considerable controversy and opposition remain. Not all states are jumping onto the community college baccalaureate bandwagon. Two states in particular, after years of discussion and debate, rejected proposals to allow their community colleges to offer four-year degrees. In 2005, Arizona came close to taking this step, when the House passed a bill that would have allowed 10 community colleges to offer four-year degrees in teacher education, health professions, law enforcement, fire services, and other workforce-related disciplines not currently offered by state universities. This bill, opposed by the state's three universities, was defeated in the Senate appropriations committee, and subsequent versions of the bill were also defeated. These actions followed debates going back to 1997, with supporters citing population growth, critical shortages in the health professions and other fields, rising university tuition, and the need to improve access for rural students. Opponents cited high start-up costs, likely increases in tuition and taxes, and threats to the traditional community college mission.

In 2009, Illinois adopted an alternative approach that favors collaboration between two- and four-year institutions. SB 1883 requires the Board of Higher Education to implement a Collaborative Baccalaureate Degree Development Grant Program "to help deliver upper-division courses and bachelor's degree programs offered by bachelor's degree-granting colleges and universities at a location geographically convenient to student populations currently being served by existing public community colleges." As background, in 2005, after years of debate, the Illinois Board of Higher Education rejected a proposal from Harper College, a two-year institution, to pilot a four-year degree program. This proposal had raised broad statewide questions and led to the creation of a Baccalaureate Access Task Force that eventually recommended against giving community colleges authority to offer baccalaureate degrees. Harper College continued to fight this battle for several years, leading to the introduction of competing bills in 2009. It was SB 1883, supported by both the Community College Board and the Board of Higher Education, which was eventually passed into law.

Substantial Variation Among States

Among states that have adopted the community college baccalaureate, approaches have varied widely. There is variation in the number and types of institutions and programs approved, and in the extent to which approved institutions retain their community college mission and culture.

Morphing Into Baccalaureate Institutions

Several states have authorized just one or two isolated community colleges to offer baccalaureate degrees, with no intention of expanding this practice to other two-year colleges in the state. Over time, such colleges have typically added more baccalaureate programs—including arts and sciences—and subsequently evolved into baccalaureate colleges, often as part of a state university system. For example:

Arkansas

Westark Community College, approved to offer its first four-year degree in 1998, became the University of Arkansas–Fort Smith in 2002. It now offers 44 baccalaureate programs, representing nearly half of all degrees conferred.

Louisiana

Louisiana State University–Alexandria, approved to offer four-year degrees in 2001, now offers 12 baccalaureate degrees, including degrees in arts and sciences, making up more than half of all degrees conferred.

Utah

Utah Valley Community College, first approved to offer a baccalaureate in 1992, became Utah Valley State College in 1993 and Utah Valley University in 2008. It now offers 53 baccalaureate programs, making up just more than half of all degrees conferred, as well as master's degrees in education, nursing, and business administration. Dixie State College of Utah, formerly Dixie Junior College (which was approved to offer four-year programs in 1999), now offers 16 four-year programs, making up a fifth of all degrees conferred annually.

West Virginia

The former Parkersburg Community College became West Virginia University at Parkersburg in 1989. It now offers 11 baccalaureate programs that make up more than a third of all degrees conferred.

New Mexico

Though not as far along in its development into a four-year institution, Northern New Mexico College, formerly Northern New Mexico Community College, is on this same pathway. Once a "normal school" that was first authorized to offer a four-year elementary education degree in 2004, it has since been approved to offer four-year degrees in all subjects, and now offers 11 such programs, making up about 15% of all degrees.

In each of the foregoing cases, the institution was allowed to grow its baccalaureate offerings. Now, these six institutions collectively account for more than 30% of such programs nationwide. Some observers would argue, in fact, that owing to their transformation, such institutions no longer belong in the discussion of the community college baccalaureate.

Multiple Institutions Maintaining Traditional Functions

A second pattern is to expand, more generally, the mission of a state's community colleges, albeit with a commitment that these institutions must maintain their traditional functions. Typically, these states view the community college as critical in meeting the state's baccalaureate needs, especially in high-demand workforce fields; the move is designed to aid place-bound adults who would otherwise have limited access to the baccalaureate. Frequently, states proceed in stages, beginning with a small number of institutions and programs, reviewing progress after some period of time, and making a further determination about continuation and expansion at a later date.

Following a comprehensive review of Washington State's educational system, convened by the governor, the state approved a pilot project in 2005 in which four community colleges were chosen to offer specialized four-year degree programs. The programs were designed to fill community needs not met by other colleges and to meet the needs of place-bound workers. In 2007, South Seattle Community College launched a bachelor of applied science (BAS) in hospitality management, Olympic College a BSN in nursing, Bellevue College a BAS in radiation and imaging sciences, and Peninsula College a BAS in applied management. Based on the success of these pilot programs, the state has since approved additional institutions and baccalaureate degree programs.

Florida stands alone in the extent to which its policy makers have recognized a direct role for community colleges in meeting the state's baccalaureate needs. This arose from concerns about critical workforce shortages in the state, especially in teacher education and nursing, and awareness that the state ranked near the bottom in baccalaureate degree production. This new role for community colleges has evolved and expanded for more than a decade, built on the explicit requirement that these colleges were not to become baccalaureate institutions. Key steps included:

- To avoid having to build new campuses to meet educational needs, a 1999 law encouraged joint baccalaureate programs between two-year colleges and universities. The law also allowed community colleges to seek approval to grant four-year degrees in areas of high demand— only as a last resort where no university was willing to establish a partnership.
- A 2001 law defined criteria for approval of community college baccalaureate programs. St. Petersburg Junior College was the first to receive such approval, and other colleges followed over the decade.
- The 2008 creation of the Florida College System made it possible that all community colleges might eventually offer the baccalaureate degree. Today, 18 of the state's 28 community colleges have been approved to offer at least one four-year degree.
- A 2009 law revised the primary mission of these colleges to include upper-level instruction and the awarding of baccalaureate degrees. It further set forth that beginning in 2010, colleges that have been offering baccalaureate programs for three years may apply to be exempt from the State Board of Education's approval for subsequent degree programs, the first time any state has made such a move.

Florida's progression thus far has generated significant concerns, especially about competition with universities and duplication of efforts. However, these misgivings have been declining to some degree as universities have faced tough budget constraints and have been unable to meet workforce demands.

The University System of Georgia classifies public institutions in the state as research universities, regional universities, state universities, state colleges, and two-year colleges. Similar to those in the Florida College System, the state colleges in Georgia are a type of hybrid institution designed to serve as associate-level access institutions and to offer limited baccalaureate programs targeted to the economic needs of their region. Macon State College, the first institution to be granted state college status (1997), now offers more than 30 four-year degree programs. Dalton State College, the second state college (1999), now offers 20 four-year degree programs. Five other associate-level institutions were approved to offer four-year degrees within the past five years, and each currently offers just a few four-year programs.

Limited Technical Degrees

A third pattern is to limit approval to applied and technical baccalaureate degrees, such as the bachelor of applied science (BAS), bachelor of applied technology (BAT), and bachelor of technology (BT) degrees. The rationale is that these represent an extension of technical programs already offered at community colleges and are designed to allow associate of applied science (AAS) graduates to further their education; four-year institutions have a shorter (or no) history with such programs.

For example, in 2002, several community colleges in Texas indicated an interest in offering the BAS and BAT degrees, arguing that the few programs of this type offered at four-year institutions were not enough to meet the needs of adult workers. In response, the legislature approved a pilot project in 2003, through which a limited number of community colleges could offer up to five BAS or BAT degrees that would correspond to the needs of local industry. The Texas Higher Education Coordinating Board (THECB) approved three colleges. A 2007 law removed the pilot status of the program, granting permanent approval to offer these programs. Further, a 2009 law directed THECB to prepare a study to examine the feasibility of expanding this to other two-year institutions. THECB issued a report to the legislature in 2010 that recommended using a variety of methods to address specific areas of need, including online education and partnerships between two- and four-year institutions (Texas Higher Education Coordinating Board, 2010). It asserted that community colleges' expansion into baccalaureate degrees should be considered only when other options have been exhausted. To date, there are only four community college baccalaureate programs established at the three institutions.

Other examples include:

Oklahoma

Oklahoma State University–Oklahoma City and Oklahoma State University Institute of Technology–Okmulgee, both associate-level colleges, offer a total of four specialized BT programs.

North Dakota

Bismarck State College offers a single four-year program, a BAS in energy management.

Others

Some states do not fit into any of the foregoing models. For example:

Nevada

Great Basin College was approved to offer four-year degrees in 1999 and now offers 13 baccalaureate programs in a variety of workforce subjects. One additional college was approved in 2004 to offer a BS in dental hygiene, and another in 2007 to offer a BT in construction management.

New York

Five of the technical colleges in the SUNY system were authorized to offer four-year degrees in 1996. They now offer a total of 84 baccalaureate programs, up from 37 programs in 2004. Though no additional colleges have been approved since then, three of these colleges have added baccalaureate-level nursing programs in recent years, a change from their traditional program offerings.

Ongoing Activity and Debate

As states grapple with ways to increase baccalaureate attainment with limited resources, there is continued interest in and controversy surrounding the community college baccalaureate. At the time of this writing, the University of Wisconsin System Board of Regents was considering action on a five-year pilot project through which six of the system's 13 two-year colleges will be able to develop limited bachelor's of applied arts and science (BAAS) degree programs. Proposed as a way to increase access to the baccalaureate for rural, place-bound adults, this concept had been in the works for several years. Though there has been some internal disagreement about potential "mission creep," no legislative approval is required, and the University of Wisconsin System has not experienced a major backlash by its four-year institutions. In fact, the programs will be developed in collaboration with partnering comprehensive universities, and the proposal was currently being vetted through faculty governance at the partner institutions. These universities will provide both on-site and online instruction, but the two-year colleges will be granting the degree, thus necessitating a mission change. The BAAS is a relatively new degree type that addresses workforce development, but in a manner that is less technical in nature than other applied baccalaureate degrees, as it emphasizes the liberal arts and their application to the work setting. Note that regents more recently approved this proposal (spring 2011).

The State of Michigan is currently embroiled in a heated debate about the community college baccalaureate. For several years, a number of community colleges have been lobbying for legislation allowing them to offer the bachelor's degree in certain technical fields, as well as the bachelor of science in nursing. Their primary arguments concern affordability and accessibility.

On the other side of the debate, the Presidents Council, representing the state's four-year universities, has lobbied hard against this proposal and instead supports the expansion of existing collaborations as the most efficient way to address workforce needs. In a letter to state representatives, the Presidents Council states: "Michigan's 15 public universities hereby pledge to collaborate with our community college colleagues to provide locally any new baccalaureate or degree completion program for which there is a demonstrated and sustainable need within that community college district. . . . This pledge by the public universities avoids duplication and waste, can be implemented immediately, and is far less costly." In September 2010, the Michigan House of Representatives passed a bill authorizing limited community college baccalaureate degrees, but the bill never received a hearing in the Senate. A bill was reintroduced during the 2011–2012 legislative session, and once again, the bill passed in the House but continues to languish in the Senate Education Committee.

A bill to authorize the Virginia Community College System to establish baccalaureate programs in nursing, education, applied technology, and other high-need areas was introduced in 2010, but was later tabled. Proponents cited this as a means to promote the governor's goal of producing 100,000 more college graduates in the state, but members of the Higher Education Subcommittee felt the legislation was premature. It was expected that the proposal would receive further consideration as part of the Governor's Commission on Higher Education: Reform, Innovation and Investment, established in 2010.

Arguments in Favor of the Community College Baccalaureate

There are a variety of compelling arguments in favor of the community college baccalaureate.

Improved Access to the Baccalaureate

Supporters argue that baccalaureate programs offered by community colleges increase educational opportunities for place-bound, adult workers, particularly in rural areas where there is no access to four-year institutions. Some argue that for first-generation college-goers and underserved groups, the opportunity to continue one's education in the familiar community college environment makes it more likely that these students will persist in college and earn a four-year degree.

Greater Affordability for Students

Though more expensive than lower-division courses, tuition for upper-division classes at community colleges is typically lower than tuition for similar courses at four-year institutions. Also, the absence of a public four-year option might lead some workers seeking baccalaureate degrees to turn to the for-profit sector, which is significantly more expensive.

Reduced Taxpayer Costs

Supporters argue that it is cheaper to offer upper-division classes at community colleges than at four-year institutions, largely because faculty are paid less and teach more, resulting in limited state dollars going farther.

Ability to Meet Local Workforce Demands

Community colleges traditionally work with local employers and develop degree and certificate programs that respond to specified workforce needs. Offering specific baccalaureate degrees in certain high-demand fields is a logical extension of this practice.

Expertise in Applied and Technical Degrees

Traditionally, applied associate degrees offered by community colleges, such as associate of applied science degrees, have been the industry standard for employment in certain technical fields. However, some high-skill occupations increasingly require a baccalaureate for job entry or promotion. Supporters argue that it makes sense to develop these degree programs where two-year programs already exist, because many four-year institutions have no history or expertise in these areas.

Overcrowding at Four-Year Colleges

In some states, demand currently exceeds capacity at four-year institutions. Offering selected baccalaureate programs at two-year colleges can help reduce overcrowding and meet regional and state workforce needs.

Arguments Against the Community College Baccalaureate

There are equally compelling arguments opposing the community college baccalaureate. As a general rule, opponents share the underlying contention that adding one more mission to community colleges is unnecessary, time-consuming, expensive, and fraught with unintended negative consequences.

Instead, they support expansion of the various models of collaboration between two-year and four-year institutions to address baccalaureate needs of the state (including university centers, shared facilities, joint programs, online education, and articulation agreements).

Mission Creep

Opponents express concern that offering baccalaureate programs at community colleges weakens the traditional community college mission and leaves behind those students it is designed to serve; this option could shift resources, raise tuition for all students, challenge open-door policies, and divert attention away from developmental education. As a worst-case scenario, the community college might morph into a four-year institution and, as a result, totally abandon the access mission.

Program Duplication

Many believe this approach produces a less-efficient state system overall, with duplication of programs offered at four-year institutions and creation of competition instead of cooperation. For example, owing to limited availability of nursing faculty and clinical sites, increasing the number of institutions with baccalaureate nursing programs could exacerbate problems rather than solve them.

Accreditation Obstacles

Attaining regional accreditation for four-year programs is both expensive and time consuming. It is far more efficient, many argue, to develop partnerships with four-year institutions that bring programs to the community college campus, thus not necessitating new accreditation.

High Costs/Need for Additional State Dollars

In order to add upper division coursework, community colleges need to upgrade faculty, libraries, and laboratories. In addition to high start-up costs, there are also high ongoing costs in terms of the employment of new categories of faculty.

Faculty Issues

Baccalaureate programs might require faculty with higher degrees who demand more pay. They could be harder to recruit and might be less focused on teaching. Rifts among the different faculty classes could develop.

Too Burdensome on Overtaxed Community Colleges

Community colleges around the nation are increasingly being asked to do more with less. Some are already over capacity and do not have the luxury of taking on more responsibilities. Some community college presidents themselves have expressed these concerns, and not all are seeking mission expansion.

Concerns About Quality

Some critics believe that a baccalaureate degree earned at a community college is inferior to one earned at a four-year institution. The belief is that courses might not be as rigorous, and faculty and resources might be substandard. Some employers share these concerns.

Availability of Online Education

Given the widespread availability of online degree programs, students are no longer limited by where they live. Adding community college baccalaureate programs might be unwarranted, especially for programs that can be effectively delivered online.

Considerations for Policy Makers

Policy makers need to weigh, in context, these pros and cons when considering the approval or expansion of community college baccalaureate programs. The key issue is whether the independently offered community college baccalaureate is the best alternative for meeting student and workforce demands, or whether it is preferable that only four-year institutions confer the baccalaureate degree. In doing so, policy makers should consider the following questions.

Cost and Finance Issues

What are the short-term costs associated with developing new community college baccalaureate degree programs?

What are the long-term costs? How will costs per degree compare with similar costs at four-year institutions?

How will the flow of state funding be affected? If they exist, do state funding formulas need to be altered?

What will the impact be on community college budgets, and how will adequate resources be found?

How will access to federal policy money be affected?

How will tuition rates be affected? Who will bear the increased costs of higher-cost programs?

Mission Issues

What is the long-term purpose of introducing baccalaureate programs into the community college environment? Will the community college be expected to maintain its traditional open access mission? Is the intention for the community college to morph into a baccalaureate institution?

How will the needs of associate-degree students and others currently being served continue to be met?

Will developmental education be protected?

Student Issues

How will chances for baccalaureate completion be affected?

Will it be cheaper or more expensive for students? Will traditionally low tuition rates be maintained for lower-division students?

Will employers accept community college baccalaureates as equal to degrees from four-year institutions?

Faculty/Staff Issues

Will new faculty need to be hired? If so, what qualifications will be sought? How will qualified faculty be attracted and retained?

How will the pay structure be affected?

Will a two-tier faculty result, and how will this affect the institution?

How can faculty and program quality be ensured?

Will additional administrative staff be needed to manage the new programs?

Conclusion

The community college baccalaureate is not a new phenomenon but one that has been growing and evolving for more than two decades. Though there has been tremendous expansion over the past 10 years, such programs are still the exception rather than the rule—often the option of last resort after other alternatives have been exhausted. The current picture is one of great variation among states in how they have implemented this practice, owing to varying demographics, workforce needs, higher education systems, fiscal conditions, and political pushback (from those opposed to the concept). Florida is at the forefront of this movement, but largely stands alone. Other states are making far more limited use of this option, or have rejected it outright.

As pressures mount to reach state and national postsecondary education goals, undoubtedly continued attention will be directed toward this phenomenon. Policy makers and campus leaders are cautioned against viewing the community college baccalaureate as a silver bullet. In considering this option, they should keep in mind the pros and cons outlined here and be alert to unintended consequences. They would be wise to proceed cautiously, following the maxim: "First, do no harm."

References

Russell, A. (2004) Update on the community college baccalaureate. *Policy matters: A higher education policy brief.* Washington, DC: American Association of State Colleges and Universities. Retrieved from http://www.congressweb.com/aascu/doc files/vIni.pdf.

Russell, A. (2010). Update on the community college baccalaureate: Evolving trends and issues. *Policy Matters: A Higher Education Policy Brief.* Washington, DC: American Association of State Colleges and Universities. Retrieved from http://www.congressweb.com/aascu/docfiles/AASCU_Update_Community_College_Baccalaureate.pdf.

Texas Higher Education Coordinating Board. (2010). *The feasibility of expanding Texas' community college baccalaureate programs: A report to the 81st legislature (Draft).* Austin, TX: author. Retrieved from http://www.thecb.state.tx.us/index .cfm?ObjectID=388644C9-B13A-773D-4C38A96B0E769BC2.

PART TWO

MODELS AND CONTEXTS

7

THE BACCALAUREATE MOVEMENT IN FLORIDA

A Decade of Change

Deborah L. Floyd and Angela M. Garcia Falconetti

Since 2000, no state has experienced more change in baccalaureate degree offerings and community colleges than the State of Florida. Florida has focused on a three-part plan to address baccalaureate degree completion—employment and workforce degrees offered by the Florida College System (FCS), partnership and concurrent use programs that result in baccalaureate degree completion, and strengthening a successful statewide articulation policy that results in university baccalaureate degree confirmation with Florida colleges as key partners. This chapter summarizes a decade of change in Florida's community colleges related to baccalaureate degree education, presents research and findings on the current status of the baccalaureate initiative, and provides perspectives on the challenges for the future.

The Evolution of the Florida Baccalaureate System

More than ten years ago, the State of Florida enacted legislation authorizing the first community college baccalaureate, with an intentioned outcome of more effectively meeting the workforce demands of employers in fields such as nursing, education, and information technology (Smith & Holcombe, 2008; Winn & Armstrong, 2005). During the ensuing ten years, Florida transitioned the Community College System to the Florida College System,

The authors are grateful to Dr. Willis Holcombe, chancellor emeritus of the Florida College System, for his contributions to this chapter.

which comprises 28 institutions, including 11 community colleges, 7 colleges, and 10 state colleges. A considerable body of literature is devoted to the development and reasons for this initiative (Barnett, 2011; FCS Annual Report, 2011; Floyd, Falconetti, & Hrabak, 2009; Floyd & Walker, 2009; Furlong, 2005; Gonzales, 2011).

In 1998 and 1999, the State Board of Community Colleges, the Postsecondary Education Planning Commission (PEPC), and the Senate Education Committee concurred that Florida community colleges were a viable option for offering baccalaureate degrees, especially in the aforementioned areas, in an effort to meet the workforce demands of the state's burgeoning population. PEPC, while recognizing the need for this new system, urged the community colleges to seek partnerships with senior institutions to offer baccalaureates rather than to confer the degrees (Floyd et al., 2009; Winn & Armstrong, 2005). Despite this recommendation, the State of Florida enacted Senate Bill (SB) 1162 (Furlong, 2005).

SB 1162 granted St. Petersburg Junior College the ability to confer baccalaureates in areas of high workforce demand and established St. Petersburg Junior College as St. Petersburg College (Furlong, 2005; Smith & Holcombe, 2008; Winn & Armstrong, 2005). Moreover, the Bill outlined the necessary steps and processes for other community colleges to pursue baccalaureates in areas that met local need and demand. These actions were followed by a study by the Board of Governors of Florida's State University System and conducted by The Pappas Consulting Group. Their recommendations noted that the development of a state college system would be a cost-effective and creative pathway to a baccalaureate education, although the report may not have envisioned the system as it has emerged. Although The Pappas Report cited Florida's community colleges as one of the vehicles for increasing baccalaureate options, it stressed that community colleges should maintain their original mission of open access (Pappas Consulting Group, 2007).

The next major legislative action was the enactment of Florida Senate Bill 1716, which passed into law on April 23, 2008. This legislation created Florida's first college system, describing it as a system of governance to "maximize open access for students, respond to community needs for postsecondary academic education, and provide associate and baccalaureate degrees that will best meet the State's employment needs" (Florida Senate Bill No. 1716, 2008). Furthermore, the bill specified that baccalaureate-granting colleges within the FCS were to provide a more cost-effective measure to the students and the state. The bill also prohibited the 28 colleges that composed the system from offering graduate credit or awarding graduate degrees (Florida Senate Bill No. 1716, 2008). Then-Governor Charlie Christ approved the legislation on May 28, 2008, and the bill officially went into effect on July 1, 2008 (Floyd et al., 2009). The bill established the Florida State College Pilot Project, which provided nine colleges with the opportunity to become state colleges: Chipola College, Daytona Beach Community College, Edison Community College, Indian River Community College, Miami-Dade Community College, Okaloosa-Walton Community College, Polk Community College, Santa Fe Community College, and St. Petersburg Junior College. Four of the nine changed their names to state colleges: Daytona State College, Edison State College, Indian River State College, and Northwest Florida State College (i.e., Okaloosa-Walton College). This trend continued throughout the state, and Florida's final junior college, Pensacola Junior College, transitioned to Pensacola State College in 2010.

As of 2011, 18 of Florida's community colleges offer baccalaureates in fields such as nursing, supervision and management, teacher education, and engineering technology. Some 2,834 students were enrolled in 2006. In three years 8,155 students enrolled for a 188% increase, demonstrating a market for these programs (Holcombe, 2010; Holcombe & Smith, 2010). The increase of baccalaureate degree granting institutions, the surge in the number of students pursuing degrees in the new system, and the integration of the colleges into the FCS is a noteworthy accomplishment that has drawn local, state, national, and international attention (Barnett, 2011; FCS Annual Report, 2011; Floyd et al., 2009; Gonzales, 2011).

The Current Status: A System in Transition

The new FCS continues the community college tradition of investing in the citizens of Florida by providing a cost-effective education that meets the needs of the workforce. Increased access to the baccalaureate is a focal point of the system, along with providing opportunities for students to improve skills through education. This occurs through joint partnerships with senior institutions, through articulation agreements, and with the direct granting of degrees. This section will cover a variety of aspects related to the baccalaureate in the new system.

First of all, who are the students? The majority of students enrolled in lower- and upper-divisions of study at the FCS are over the age of 24, in contrast to the students enrolled in baccalaureate programs of the State University System (SUS), who are younger than 24. In the FCS, 45.4% of lower-division enrollees and 74.5% of upper-division students are over the age of 24. Within the SUS, 81.4% of upper-division enrollees are 24 or younger. These statistics indicate that the FCS attracts an older student population, carrying on the tradition of community colleges that has always attracted an older student population (figure 7.1).

Additionally, since the inception of the baccalaureates in Florida in 2000, enrollment in upper-division course work added to the overall enrollment in the FCS. Table 7.1 illustrates the changes in head count, the 2010 enrollment in upper-division course work, and the changes in the names of Florida's colleges between the years of 2000 and 2010.

Of Florida's 28 colleges, 20 changed names; henceforth, eliminating the term *community* from the name. The enrollment of the FCS, since 2000, increased by 181,062 students (i.e., $n = 700,467$ to $n = 881,529$), representing 12,408 students enrolled in upper-division course work. Interestingly, St. Johns River State College and Miami Dade College enrolled the greatest number of students ($n = 4,486$; $n = 2,240$, respectively) in upper-division course work in 2010. Seminole State College of Florida ($n = 26$) and State College of Florida, Manatee-Sarasota ($n = 46$) enrolled the fewest students in upper-division course work.

FIGURE 7.1
A Comparison of Ages of Students Enrolled in the SUS and the FCS

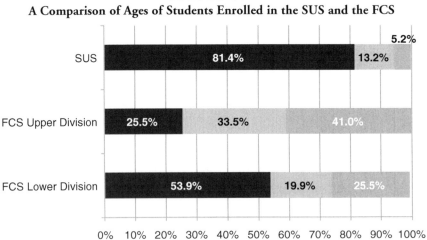

TABLE 7.1

FCS College Name Changes and Enrollment Between 2000 and 2010

College Name			Enrollment 2010	
2000	2010	Enrollment 2000	Lower Division	Upper Division
Brevard Community College	Brevard Community College	25,472	28,659	—
Broward Community College	Broward College	45,641	60,315	414
Central Florida Community College	College of Central Florida	16,594	16,795	—
Chipola Junior College	Chipola College	5,462	4,600	232
Daytona Beach Community College	Daytona State College	29,327	35,441	934
Edison Community College	Edison State College	20,305	24,117	710
Florida Community College at Jacksonville	Florida State College at Jacksonville	54,639	84,305	816
Florida Keys Community College	Florida Keys Community College	3,721	3,115	—
Gulf Coast Community College	Gulf Coast State College*	20,609	21,815	—
Hillsborough Community College	Hillsborough Community College	35,291	45,494	—
Indian River Community College	Indian River State College	38,964	33,433	1,158
Lake City Community College	Florida Gateway College	5,625	5,674	—
Lake-Sumter Community College	Lake-Sumter Community College	6,045	8,800	—
Manatee Community College	State College of Florida, Manatee-Sarasota	16,147	23,336	46
Miami Dade Community College	Miami Dade College	97,223	134,005	2,240
North Florida Community College	North Florida Community College	4,121	2,285	—

(continues)

TABLE 7.1 (Continued)

College Name		Enrollment 2000	Enrollment 2010	
2000	2010		Lower Division	Upper Division
Okaloosa-Walton Community College	Northwest Florida State College	13,368	14,560	607
Palm Beach Community College	Palm Beach State College	35,937	49,904	422
Pasco-Hernando Community College	Pasco-Hernando Community College	10,239	17,422	—
Pensacola Junior College	Pensacola State College*	22,723	22,463	—
Polk Community College	Polk State College	18,202	19,407	136
St. Johns River Community College	St. Johns River State College*	8,235	10,833	4,486
St. Petersburg Junior College	St. Petersburg College	47,102	52,698	—
Santa Fe Community College	Santa Fe College	20,654	24,162	181
Seminole Community College	Seminole State College of Florida	20,974	30,063	26
South Florida Community College	South Florida Community College	7,010	9,040	—
Tallahassee Community College	Tallahassee Community College	20,182	36,264	—
Valencia Community College*	Valencia College*	50,655	62,524	—
Florida Community College System	**Florida College System**	**700,467**	**881,529**	**12,408**

*Name change effective 2011.

St. Petersburg College offers the majority of baccalaureates (i.e., 23). As noted previously, St. Petersburg College was also the first institution to confer baccalaureates per the enacting legislation of SB 1162 in 2001. Miami Dade College is second in the hierarchy of number of degrees offered at 13. Miami Dade and Chipola College are the only two colleges that began offering baccalaureates in 2002. By 2002, three colleges offered baccalaureate degrees: St. Petersburg College, Miami Dade College, and Chipola College. Table 7.2 notes the number of baccalaureates offered, the dates of inception, and the type of baccalaureate offered by college of the FCS.

The majority of students, from 2003–2004 to 2009–2010, enrolled in baccalaureate of applied science (BAS) degrees. Five hundred and eleven students enrolled in BAS degrees in 2003–2004 and 8,044 in 2009–2010, representing a growth of 7,533 in student enrollment in BAS programs in seven years. The difference in number of students enrolled in baccalaureates between 2003–2004 and 2009–2010 is 11,940, with a total baccalaureate enrollment of 13,168 in 2009–2010. Figure 7.2 represents baccalaureate enrollments by type of program. The numbers reflect students enrolled in a program. Students admitted to the upper division but not in a program are excluded.

Students enrolled in the BAS degrees of the FCS enrolled in specialized disciplines, as noted between the years of 2005–2006 and 2009–2010 in table 7.3. The SUS solely offers a BAS program in supervision and management as compared with the FCS, which offers 16 BAS programs. The University of Central Florida has the only active BAS program in the SUS. The University of South Florida and Florida Gulf Coast University offer a bachelor of science in applied science. Other universities offer articulation for applied science degrees. The number of students enrolled in BAS programs of the FCS increased by 6,835 between the academic years of 2005–2006 and 2009–2010. The majority of students ($n=1,051$), in 2009–2010, were enrolled in public safety management (table 7.3).

The preceding figures and graphs illustrate the growth of the baccalaureate offerings through the colleges affiliated with the FCS. This growth, however, is just part of the story. Partnerships with senior institutions and articulation agreements with universities and colleges offer another avenue for students seeking the baccalaureate as well.

Postsecondary Partnerships of Concurrent- and Joint-Use Programs

Baccalaureate degree offerings through partnership models, such as university centers and articulation models are among the most popular delivery

TABLE 7.2
The Status of FCS Baccalaureates

College	*Number of Baccalaureate Degrees Offered*	*Dates of Inception of Baccalaureate Degrees*	*Baccalaureate Degrees and Major Fields*
Broward College (formerly Broward Community College)	9 degrees offered since 2008	2008	BS Exceptional Student Education; Middle Grades Mathematics; Secondary Mathematics; Middle Grades Science; Secondary Biology; Secondary Mathematics
		2009	BS Nursing BAS Information Management; Supervision and Management; Technology Management
Chipola College (formerly Chipola Junior College)	10 degrees offered since 2002	2002	BS Middle Grades Mathematics; Middle Grades Science; Secondary Science-Biology; Secondary Mathematics Education
		2007	BAS Organizational Management
		2008	BS Elementary Education; Exceptional Student Education; Nursing
		2010	BS Business Administration; Secondary English Education

TABLE 7.2 (Continued)

College	Number of Baccalaureate Degrees Offered	Dates of Inception of Baccalaureate Degrees	Baccalaureate Degrees and Major Fields
College of Central Florida (formerly Central Florida Community College)	2 degrees offered since 2010	2010	BAS Business and Organizational Management BS Early Childhood Education, Pre-K through Grade 3
Daytona State College (formerly Daytona Beach Community College and Daytona Beach College)	9 degrees offered since 2005	2005	BAS Supervision and Management
		2008	BS Elementary Education; Exceptional Student Education; Secondary Mathematics; Secondary Biology; Secondary Chemistry; Secondary Physics; Secondary Earth/Space Science
		2010	BS Engineering Technology
Edison State College (formerly Edison Community College)	10 degrees offered since 2005	2005	BAS Public Safety Management
		2007	BS Secondary Mathematics; Secondary Biology
		2008	BS Elementary Education; Nursing BAS Supervision and Management

TABLE 7.2 (Continued)

College	Number of Baccalaureate Degrees Offered	Dates of Inception of Baccalaureate Degrees	Baccalaureate Degrees and Major Fields
		2010	BS
			Middle Grades Language Arts; Middle Grades Mathematics; Middle Grades Science
			BAS
			Cardiopulmonary Sciences
Florida Gateway College (formerly Lake City Community College)	1 degree in 2011	2011	BS
			Nursing
Florida State College at Jacksonville (formerly Florida Junior College and Florida Community College at Jacksonville)	9 degrees offered since 2006	2006	Fire Science Management
		2008	BS
			Computer Networking; Nursing
			BAS
			Supervision and Management
		2009	BS
			Early Childhood Education, Age 3 through Grade 3; Information Technology Management; Public Safety Management
		2010	BS
			Biomedical Sciences; Business Administration
		2011	BAS
			Digital Media
Gulf Coast State College (formerly Gulf Coast Community College)	1 degree in 2010	2010	BAS
			Technology Management

TABLE 7.2 (Continued)

College	Number of Baccalaureate Degrees Offered	Dates of Inception of Baccalaureate Degrees	Baccalaureate Degrees and Major Fields
Indian River State College (formerly Indian River Community College)	10 degrees offered since 2007	2007	BS Exceptional Student Education; Middle Grades Mathematics; Middle Grades Science; Nursing; Secondary Biology; Secondary Mathematics BAS Organizational Management
		2010	BS Biology; Human Services BAS Digital Media
State College of Florida, Manatee-Sarasota (formerly Manatee Community College)	5 degrees offered since 2010	2009	BS Nursing
		2010	BS Early Childhood Education BAS Energy Technology Management; Health Services Administration; Public Safety Administration/ Homeland Security
Miami Dade College (formerly Miami Beach Community College)	14 degrees offered since 2002	2002	BS Exceptional Student Education; Secondary Biology; Secondary Chemistry; Secondary Physics; Secondary Earth Science; Secondary Mathematics
		2006	BAS Public Safety

TABLE 7.2 (Continued)

College	Number of Baccalaureate Degrees Offered	Dates of Inception of Baccalaureate Degrees	Baccalaureate Degrees and Major Fields
		2007	BS Nursing
		2009	BAS Film, Television, and Digital Production; Health Science; Supervision and Management
		2010	BS Electronics Engineering Technology
		2011	BS Biological Sciences; Early Childhood Education
Northwest Florida State College (formerly Okaloosa-Walton Community College)	5 degrees offered since 2003	2003	BAS Project Management
		2007	BS Elementary Education
		2008	BS Nursing
		2009	BS Middle Grades Math; Middle Grades Science
Palm Beach State College (formerly Palm Beach Community College)	3 degrees offered since 2008	2008	BAS Supervision and Management
		2010	BS Nursing BAS Information Technology

TABLE 7.2 (Continued)

College	Number of Baccalaureate Degrees Offered	Dates of Inception of Baccalaureate Degrees	Baccalaureate Degrees and Major Fields
Pensacola State College (formerly Pensacola Junior College)	2 degrees offered in 2010	2010	BS Nursing BAS Administration and Supervision
Polk State College (formerly Polk Community College)	2 degrees offered since 2009	2009	BAS Supervision and Management
		2011	BS Nursing
Santa Fe College (formerly Santa Fe Community College)	3 degrees offered since 2009	2009	BAS Clinical Laboratory Science; Health Science Administration
		2011	BS Early Childhood Education, Birth through Age 4, non-certification
Seminole State College of Florida (formerly Seminole Community College)	6 degrees offered since 2009	2009	BAS Interior Design
		2010	BS Architectural Engineering Technology; Business Information Management; Construction; Information Systems Technology; Early Childhood Education, Birth through Age 4, non-certification
St. Johns River State College (formerly St. Johns River Community College)	2 degrees offered since 2010	2010	BS Early Childhood Education BAS Organizational Management

TABLE 7.2 (Continued)

College	Number of Baccalaureate Degrees Offered	Dates of Inception of Baccalaureate Degrees	Baccalaureate Degrees and Major Fields
St. Petersburg College (formerly St. Petersburg Community College)	24 degrees offered since 2001	2001	BS Elementary Education; Exceptional Student Education; Nursing; Secondary Mathematics; Secondary Biology BAS Technology Management
		2003	BAS Dental Hygiene; Orthotics and Prosthetics; Public Safety Management
		2004	BS Secondary Business Technology Education; Secondary Technology Education; Veterinary Technology
		2005	BAS International Business; Paralegal Studies
		2006	BAS Banking
		2007	BS Educational Studies—non-certification BAS Health Services Administration; Management and Organizational Leadership; Middle Grades Mathematics; Middles Grades Science; Sustainability Management

TABLE 7.2 (Continued)

College	Number of Baccalaureate Degrees Offered	Dates of Inception of Baccalaureate Degrees	Baccalaureate Degrees and Major Fields
		2008	BS
			Biology, General; Business Administration; Public Policy and Administration
State College of Florida, Manatee-Sarasota (formerly Manatee Community College)	7 degrees offered since 2009	2009	BS
			Nursing
		2010	BS
			Early Childhood Education, Birth to Age 4, non-certification; Electrical and Computer Engineering Technology; Radiologic and Imaging Sciences
			BAS
			Energy Technology Management; Health Services Administration; Public Safety Management/Homeland Security

modes in the United States (Floyd, 2005) and are important to the FCS baccalaureate delivery focus. Florida's concurrent-use and joint-use partnership offerings have steadily grown along with the new community college baccalaureate degree offerings. Since 2000–2001, such concurrent- and joint-use partnerships provided opportunities for students to complete degrees on the college campus, yet the degree was awarded by the partnering institution (Concurrent Use Partnerships, 2010).

In 2010, 26 of Florida's 28 colleges partnered with 9 of the 11 public state universities, 9 independent universities, and 6 state colleges and universities. The 28 colleges of the FCS provided access to 409 upper-level baccalaureate programs, 134 master's programs, 5 specialist programs, 11 doctoral programs, and 6 professional programs on Florida College System campuses or shared facilities (Concurrent Use Partnerships, 2010). The total number of concurrent-use and joint-use partnerships increased by 141% since 2000–2001, from 234 to 565 (figure 7.3).

FIGURE 7.2
FCS Baccalaureate Enrollment Between 2003 and 2010

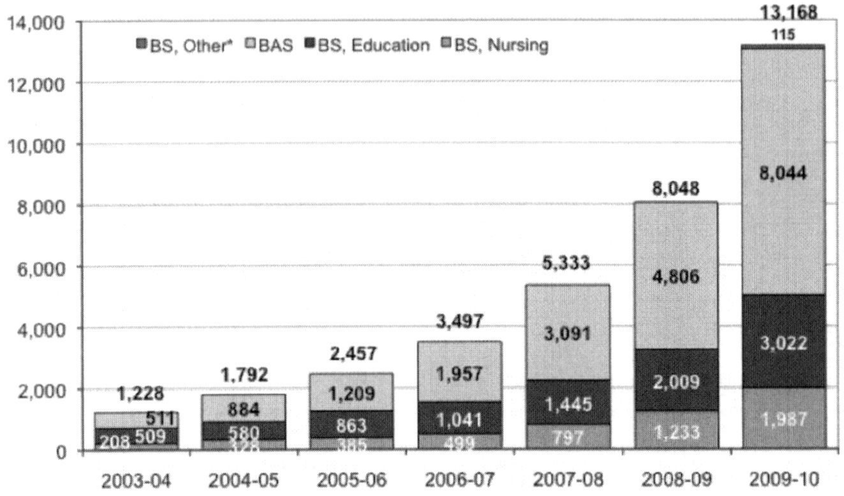

*BS, Biology and BS, Business

The institutions that reported enrollment in such programs increased by 62% from 12,747 to 20,582 (figure 7.4) (Concurrent Use Partnerships, 2010).

The top four partnership degree program areas were education, business, the health professions, and liberal arts. Psychology and public administration tied for fifth. The number of programs offered by colleges and universities are noted in table 7.4 (Concurrent Use Partnerships, 2010).

Florida's Statewide 2 + 2 Articulation Policy

Concurrently with the growth of new baccalaureate degree programs, Florida's colleges also strengthened statewide articulation policies with universities. The purpose of Florida's statewide articulation agreement is to facilitate the efficient and effective transfer of students and to provide students with the opportunity to attain their educational objectives as quickly as circumstances permit (Florida Statute Section 1007.01, 2004). Florida's 2 + 2 policy defines the earning of a baccalaureate as the successful completion of 60 credit hours at a community college, college, or state college and the remaining courses at a university. Although the expected time to degree completion

TABLE 7.3

A Comparison of FCS and SUS Enrollment in BAS Programs Between 2005–2006 and 2009–2010

Enrollments	2005–06		2006–07		2007–08		2008–09		2009–10	
	FCS	SUS	FCS	SUS	FCS	SUS	FCS	SUS	FCS	SUS
Supervision and Management	13	20	213	41	811	60	1,949	84	4,171	
International Business	103	—	196	—	264	—	276	—	264	
Public Safety Management	89	—	353	—	651	—	885	—	1,051	
Dental Hygiene	137	—	161	—	191	—	213	—	178	
Orthotics and Prosthetics	23	—	45	—	47	—	42	—	51	
Fire Science Management	—	—	—	—	6	—	12	—	17	
Computer Networking	—	—	—	—	—	—	77	—	141	
Veterinary Technology	81	—	125	—	126	—	151	—	169	
Technology Management	514	—	515	—	500	—	451	—	439	
Banking	—	—	28	—	66	—	97	—	103	
Project and Acquisitions Management	221	—	240	—	279	—	334	—	464	
Interdisciplinary Health and Human Studies	—	—	—	—	37	—	205	—	671	
Paralegal Studies	28	—	81	—	113	—	148	—	184	
Clinical Laboratory Science	—	—	—	—	—	—	—	—	29	
Sustainability Management	—	—	—	—	—	—	—	—	79	
Interior Design	—	—	—	—	—	—	—	—	33	
Total	1,209	20	1,957	41	3,091	60	4,840	84	8,044	

FIGURE 7.3
FCS and SUS Concurrent-Use and Joint-Use Partnerships
Between 2000 and 2011

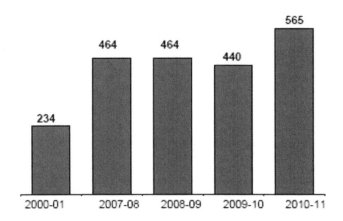

Self-Reported Concurrent-Use Partnerships
Number of Programs Offered

FIGURE 7.4
Enrollment in Concurrent-Use and Joint-Use Partnerships
Between 2000 and 2011

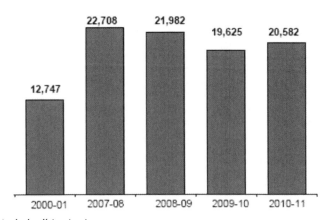

Self-Reported Enrollment in Partnership Programs*

*May not include all institutions.

TABLE 7.4
FCS Baccalaureate Program Type and Number of Programs

Type of Program	# of Programs
Education	129
Business, Management, Marketing, and Related Support Services	126
Health Professions and Related Clinical Sciences	43
Liberal Arts and Sciences, General Studies and Humanities	34
Psychology	33
Public Administration and Social Service Professions	33
Security and Protective Services	25
Visual and Performing Arts	21
Social Sciences	20
Computer and Information Sciences and Support Services	15
Engineering Technologies/Technicians	11
Engineering	11
Legal Professions and Studies	11
Communication, Journalism, and Related Programs	8
Parks, Recreation, Leisure, and Fitness Studies	6
Professional Studies	6
Agriculture, Agriculture Operations, and Related Sciences	6
Biological and Biomedical Sciences	5
Architecture and Related Services	4
Multi/Interdisciplinary Studies	3
Natural Resources and Conservation	3
Aviation and Airway Management and Operations	3
English Language and Literature/Letters	2
Family and Consumer Sciences/Human Sciences	2
Area, Ethnic, Cultural, and Gender Studies	1
History	1
Library Science	1

accrues to 120 credit hours, universities may request permission of their boards of trustees to create programs in excess of 120 hours.

The dramatic growth in FCS enrollments is proportionally increasing the number of associate in arts (AA) graduates. A gap is growing between the number of AA graduates seeking to transfer and transfer admissions to the SUS. While the statewide articulation agreement exists, universities may request of the respective board of trustees to limit access to selected academic programs, hence, decreasing the number of programs to which AA graduates of the

FCS may transfer. State universities will need to increase the number of transfer students admitted to the upper level of study at the universities to meet the demand for junior level AA transfers (figure 7.5).

With more students choosing to pursue the baccalaureate through one of the avenues afforded by the colleges in the FCS (i.e., articulation, partnerships, new baccalaureate degree offerings), major shifts will continue in the entire higher education system in the state.

A Final Question: What Does This Mean?

For some time the debate raged over whether community colleges should offer the baccalaureate. In Florida, the debate is moot at this time. Florida developed and accepted this new system, and although some may rightly argue that this change occurred more as a matter of politics than as an educational master plan, it has become a reality (Barnett, 2011). These "new colleges" are here, and evidence exists that the colleges are "making a difference" by addressing workforce needs in the local communities.

Moreover, as higher education becomes more expensive for students pursuing a degree, there may be more students who choose to attend a college close to home. This has long been the mantra of community colleges in attracting students to their two-year degree programs. It seems a natural progression for advancing a cause for attaining a baccalaureate at a college close to home, especially in a workforce-related field leading directly to employment. The cost to students and taxpayers is less for obtaining a baccalaureate degree through a college in the FCS as compared to costs of a university in the SUS.

There are questions regarding the relationships between the FCS and the SUS on a variety of issues that will need to be addressed in due time. How will the SUS view graduates from these new programs? Will baccalaureate degree graduates of the FCS programs be regarded by employers as equal to students graduating from an SUS institution? Will university graduate schools readily accept Florida college baccalaureate degrees for graduate studies? Will the SUS encourage the FCS to develop new programs that the SUS considers their territory? Already some of the SUS institutions are opposing certain programs being adopted at specific FCS schools. What is important is that the state and local policy makers, including those of the FCS and SUS, must initiate open discussions on these issues as new models for baccalaureate delivery emerge.

FIGURE 7.5
FCS Transfer Students to the SUS

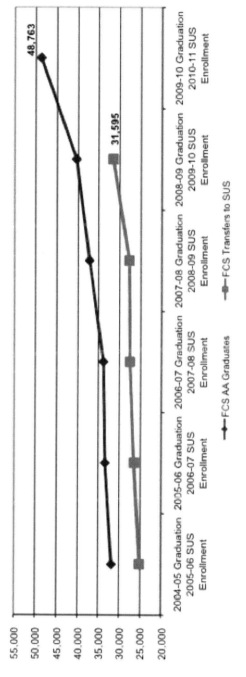

48,763

31,595

2004-05 Graduation   2005-06 Graduation   2006-07 Graduation   2007-08 Graduation   2008-09 Graduation   2009-10 Graduation
2005-06 SUS   2006-07 SUS   2007-08 SUS   2008-09 SUS   2009-10 SUS   2010-11 SUS
Enrollment   Enrollment   Enrollment   Enrollment   Enrollment   Enrollment

55,000
50,000
45,000
40,000
35,000
30,000
25,000
20,000

—♦—FCS AA Graduates   —■—FCS Transfers to SUS

Other questions are equally important. How will these new colleges be assessed? How will their graduates be recognized? What will the cost of the new system be to the State of Florida? Can the FCS colleges afford this new mission? Will the open door community college mission still be a priority? These are just a few of the challenges of accountability and mission in need of attention going forward.

A recent article in *Florida Trend* magazine noted that "while the system may be in flux, some things have not changed: Florida still ranks low in producing bachelor's degrees . . . 41st in the nation. As Floyd said, "We are not at risk of overeducating Floridians" (Barnett, 2011, p. 82). The new FCS can be the vehicle for change that can positively impact the workforce needs of the state, ensuring that Florida has an educated citizenry that will flourish in the 21st century. The Florida transition to address increasing baccalaureate attainment "is the bellwether" (Floyd, as cited in Barnett, 2011) as this well-established community college system expands the focus to address issues and challenges of increasing the baccalaureate attainment of Floridians (Barnett, 2011, p. 79). The changes in Florida will be watched closely by educators and legislators across the country and beyond as this three-pronged approach emphasis to baccalaureate delivery evolves.

References

Barnett, C. (2011, July). A mission leap for Florida's Colleges: Is the new Florida College System cutting-edge or overreaching? *Florida Trend: The Magazine of Florida Business* 54(4), 78–82.

Concurrent Use Partnerships. (2010). *Access to the baccalaureate: Concurrent-use and joint-use partnerships between the Florida College System and universities/and colleges.* Tallahassee: Florida Department of Education, The Florida College System.

Florida College System. (2010). *The Florida College System business plan 2011–2012.* Retrieved from http://www.fldoe.org/cc/pdf/FCS_BusinessPlan.pdf

FCS Annual Report. (2011). *The Florida College System annual report 2011.* Retrieved from http://www.fldoe.org/cc/pdf/annualreport2011.pdf

FCS Baccalaureate Status. (2011). Florida Department of Education, The Florida College System, Tallahassee, Florida.

Florida Senate Bill No. 1162. (2001). Retrieved from http://www.leg.state.fl.us/cgibin/view_page.pl?Tab = session&Submenu = 1&FT = D&File = sb1162er.html &Directory = session/2001/Senate/bills/billtext/html/

Florida Senate Bill No. 1716. (2008). Retrieved from http://www.flsenate.gov/cgibin/view_page.pl?Tab = session&Submenu = 1&FT = D&File = sb1716er.html&Directory = session/2008/Senate/bills/billt ext/html/

Florida Statute 1007.01. (2004). Articulation; legislative intent; purpose, role of the State Board of Education. Retrieved from http://www.hccfl.edu/sacs/draft_report/documents/FSgenedrule.pdf

Floyd, D. L. (2005). The community college baccalaureate in the U.S. In D. L. Floyd, M. L. Skolnik, & K. P. Walker (Eds.), *The community college baccalaureate: Emerging trends and policy issues* (pp. 25–47). Sterling, VA: Stylus.

Floyd, D. L., Falconetti, A. M. G., & Hrabak, M. R. (2009). Baccalaureate community colleges: The new Florida College System. *Community College Journal of Research and Practice, 33*(2), 195–202.

Floyd, D. L., & Walker, K. P. (2009). The community college baccalaureate: Putting the pieces together. *Community College Journal of Research and Practice, 33*(2), 90–124.

Furlong, T. E. (2005). St. Petersburg College: Increasing access in critical areas. In D. L. Floyd, M. L. Skolnik, & K. P. Walker, (Eds.), *The community college baccalaureate: Emerging trends and policy issues* (pp. 103–127). Sterling, VA: Stylus.

Gonzales, J. (2011). Go to community college, earn a bachelor's degree: Florida likes that combination. *The Chronicle of Higher Education,* June 12. Retrieved from http://chronicle.com/article/Floridas-CommunityColleges/127880/?key = SGM nKF5pbiAVYy4wNj5KYW5RO3Q8NkJ7YXNIaCoubl5dEg%3D%3D

Holcombe, W. N. (2010, May). *To benefit our state: Baccalaureate degrees in the Florida College System.* Presentation at the National Institute for Staff and Organizational Development's annual meeting, Austin, TX.

Holcombe, W. N., & Smith, E. J. (2010). *Baccalaureate program trends and accountability* (Program Review). Retrieved from the Florida Department of Education website: http://www.fldoe.org/cc/osas/evaluations/pdf/fyi2010-02.pdf

Pappas Consulting Group. (2007). *Proposing a blueprint for higher education in Florida: Outlining the way to a long-term master plan for higher education in Florida.* Tallahassee, FL: Pappas Consulting Group.

Smith, E. J., & Holcombe, W. N. (2008). *Baccalaureate programs in community colleges.* Retrieved from http://www.fldoe.org/cc/Vision/PDFs/PR2008_02_Baccalaureate_Program_Review.pdf The Florida College System.

Winn, J., & Armstrong, J. D. (2005). *Community college baccalaureate document inventory.* Retrieved from http://www.fldoe.org/cc/students/pdf/HistBacc.pdf

8

APPLIED BACCALAUREATE DEGREES IN THE CONTEXT OF BACCALAUREATE EDUCATION

Collin M. Ruud and Debra D. Bragg

The bachelor's degree has been long seen as the standard in postsecondary education, leading graduates to a multitude of careers following graduation. As a result, baccalaureate degrees are the most popular postsecondary degrees awarded, with U.S. institutions awarding more than 1.5 million of them in 2010. This number is more than all other degree levels (associate's, master's, and doctoral) combined (Chronicle of Higher Education, 2010). Employers have largely driven this increase in demand. Many positions now require the bachelor's degree, especially those that offer stable income growth and are widely sought nationally (e.g., teachers, businesspeople, information technologists, and others). According to the National Center for Education Statistics (NCES) (2009), enrollment growth between 1987 and 1997 was 14%, and between 1997 and 2007, was 26%. Furthermore, it is anticipated that future growth in postsecondary markets is likely to occur among adults, rather than within the traditional college-age population. According to NCES, enrollments from 2006 to 2017 will rise 10% among individuals under the age of 25, but 19% among individuals age 25 and over (2009).

These shifts are attributable to several factors. The first is that enrollment rates for traditional college-age individuals are already high when compared with the adult population. At present, adults make up a smaller proportion of total enrollments but make up a much larger segment of the U.S. population. A second factor leading to increasing enrollment growth for older adults includes increased expectations and requirements for career paths and job promotion. More jobs currently require at least a baccalaureate degree, and many career paths can "dead-end" employees who do not have a bachelor's degree, requiring them to finish such degrees in order to seek and receive promotion (Osborne, Marks, & Turner, 2004). As a result, a greater number of adults, who are also full-time employees, geographically place-bound, and dealing with work and familial responsibilities at home are actively seeking a baccalaureate education.

It is difficult for baccalaureate degree-granting institutions to keep up with this demand, in several ways. The first is simply capacity. In Florida, for example, the community college baccalaureate has become a prominent facet of public postsecondary education, in part owing to four-year institutions being unable to keep up with the increasing demand for baccalaureate degree programs. The second is that these new incoming students require a whole host of different services. As full-time employees, they often require courses that are either asynchronous or offered on nights and weekends. As place-bound individuals with families, they often require online or distance education options in order to complete course work and attend "class." As adults with additional responsibilities, they often require support that is able to adapt to their specific needs, both academically and psychologically (Levin, 2007).

All of these pressures for access to and success in baccalaureate degree programs are coupled with the U.S. political and economic atmosphere that is pressing for development and expansion of its workforce and an increase in the number of college graduates in the nation. Likely at the forefront of this push are the challenges put forth by President Obama, who called for the United States to become the nation with the highest proportion of college-educated citizens through broad changes to economic and educational policies. Furthermore, Obama's American Graduation Initiative sought to improve education particularly in high-demand workforce fields, by supporting the development of educational facilities and creation of online programs that would better facilitate education, particularly to geographically place-bound and low-income individuals who desire a postsecondary credential (Schoeff, 2009).

One particular type of baccalaureate degree that has experienced some growth the past few decades has been the applied baccalaureate (AB) degree. The AB degree, for the purpose of this discussion, is defined as a degree that incorporates applied course work and integrates higher-order thinking skills and other skills necessary for employment. Referencing state legislation, some scholars (see, for example, Floyd & Walker, 2009) have argued AB degrees are workforce-centered baccalaureate degrees, taking occupational and technical course work obtained with an applied associate's degree and applying additional technical courses to fulfill baccalaureate degree requirements. Our research confirms these forms of AB exist, but our national studies have also located AB degrees that integrate a liberal arts focus, broadening the students' learning and pursuits beyond employment. Anecdotally, graduates of AB programs have been able to expand their career opportunities or move upward in their current careers, moving into higher-paying positions as well as management roles.

Methods and Results

This research on AB degrees began in 2007, with the awarding of a grant from Lumina Foundation for Education. Research followed a two-phase process in order to gain both a larger contextual view of AB degrees nationally as well as a view of the institutional, local, regional, and statewide contexts in regard to AB degrees within a few representative states. Our understandings of these degrees were fairly limited when research began in 2007, so we proceeded to conduct a relatively exhaustive review of the literature. Most research that addressed AB degrees were within a larger context: technical degrees (Ignash & Kotun, 2005), community college baccalaureate (CCB) degrees (Floyd, Skolnik, & Walker, 2005), and in several cases we were able to find state policy or legislative documents that made limited reference to such degrees, such as the Cherry Commission's (2004) report to Michigan on improving college completion, and the Kentucky Council on Postsecondary Education's report on completion degrees. However, there was still a limited understanding of the scope and breadth of these degrees nationally, as well as of the specific state policy contexts that preceded the development and implementation of AB degrees.

Phase One Research

The first phase of research was the design, implementation, and analysis of a national inventory of AB degrees in the public sector (Townsend, Bragg, & Ruud, 2008). Researchers from the University of Missouri and the University of Illinois first conducted a Web scan, using online search engines, institutional websites, LexisNexis, and other online databases to identify public two- or four-year institutions that awarded AB degrees or had existing AB programs. This preliminary search allowed us to tailor our inventory methodology whenever information was available on programs and states.

Following the preliminary search, researchers developed an inventory questionnaire that contained broad questions regarding the existence and implementation of AB degrees. The instrument was designed to be addressed by state-level administrators responsible for higher education in the state, or for institutional administrators in states where institutions were not governed or coordinated by a statewide board. The inventory included questions such as "Are there any public institutions that award AB degrees in your state?" "When were AB degrees first implemented in your state, and where?" "Was there any state-level effort that encouraged or facilitated the development of AB degrees in your state?" "Is there any legislation that addresses the AB degree in your state?" and "How strong, in regards to enrollment, are these degrees in your state?"

The inventory questionnaires were filled out using information from the preliminary search when available. Respondents, typically state-level administrators responsible for academic affairs or approval of degree programs in the state, were identified through websites, search engines, and the advice of our advisory group. When we had identified individuals from all 50 states, inventory questionnaires were sent to all individuals to review and fill out as necessary. Where possible, we asked to follow up via telephone with these individuals in order to discuss AB degrees and the state policy context at greater length.

Responses were received from at least one individual in all 50 states, giving us a 100% response rate for states. Most of the respondents were able to follow up over the telephone, but a few officials, particularly those in states with no AB degree programs in any of the public institutions, responded with the requested information but did not agree to a phone conversation. Where possible, researchers filled in all of the information requested through the questionnaires either through e-mail responses or phone conversations, to give us a complete idea of these degrees across the nation. Data were then used to generate a national inventory of AB degree programs in the United States, as well as some preliminary policy information that better helped us understand the contexts surrounding the creation and implementation of AB degree programs nationally.

Phase One Results

The results of the first phase of research were compiled into a table as well as a national map, documenting which states had AB degrees, the number of public institutions within the states that awarded such degrees, and whether the state had AB degrees at either the two-year or four-year institutional level or at both levels. As of 2008, when the inventory was published, AB degrees were offered in the public sector at 39 of 50 states. Of these 39 states, 10 had public two-year as well as four-year institutions that awarded AB degrees, based on our definition (mentioned earlier in this chapter). Apart from New York in the 1970s and early 1980s, no state was recorded as having AB degrees at only the two-year institutional level, so the other 29 states had only four-year public institutions that offered the AB degree. See figure 8.1 and table 8.1 for more information from the inventory.

In addition to the inventory report (Townsend et al., 2008), researchers released a policy brief (Bragg, Townsend, & Ruud, 2009), detailing additional information reported during telephone interviews with state officials regarding the development and implementation of AB degrees in their particular states. One finding showed commonalities between states when respondents were asked to discuss what prompted the development of AB degrees. Several state officials named a number of distinct reasons for increasing the demand for AB degrees in their states. The first reason was a need to increase baccalaureate degree completion. Although many state officials had noted that this was a direct response to pressure from politicians and other state leaders to increase baccalaureate productivity in the state, other reasons for increasing baccalaureate completion rates were to improve economic conditions in-state, increase competitiveness between states and internationally, and to promote growth in certain job markets and career fields, such as fields in science, technology, engineering, and mathematics (STEM).

Another impetus behind the development of AB degrees found during the first phase of research was the need to improve transfer in-state. In several states that did not offer AB degrees in the public sector, state officials would note a lower number of associate's degree graduates annually than the state was expected to produce or than what was needed in the labor market. Furthermore, some of these officials would also note that those students who pursued associate's degrees would typically acquire traditional transfer degrees, affording them routes to the baccalaureate that have been struck through existing articulation agreements between community colleges and universities. In several states with AB degrees, increased demand from associate's degree holders and employers often facilitated the development of AB degrees. With a large number of individuals with applied associate's degrees unable to transfer into baccalaureate programs, it seemed logical that these

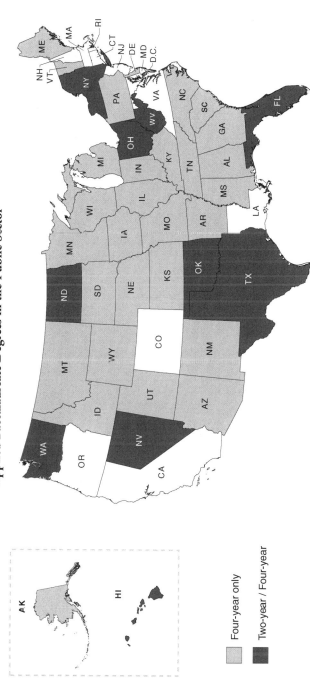

FIGURE 8.1
Applied Baccalaureate Degrees in the Public Sector

☐ Four-year only

■ Two-year / Four-year

Note. Adapted from Townsend, B. K., Bragg, D. D., & Ruud, C. M. (2008). *The adult learner and the applied baccalaureate: National and state-by-state inventory.* Retrieved from http://occrl.illinois.edu/files/Projects/lumina/Report/App3accInventory.pdf

TABLE 8.1
Applied Baccalaureate Degrees in the Public Sector

State	Any AB	4Y AB	2Y AB	Prior CCB	AB Legislated	Accreditor	# AB 2Y	# AB 4Y	Decade Imp.	AB Degree Designation
AL	✓	✓				SACS	0	1	1970	BAS
AK	✓	✓				NWCCU	0	1	1990	BST
AZ	✓	✓			✓	NCA-HLC	0	4	1990	BAS
AR	✓	✓		✓	✓	NCA-HLC	0	4	1990	BAS
CA										
CO										
CT										
DE	✓	✓				MSCHE	0	1	1980	BAS
FL	✓	✓	✓		✓	SACS	9	2	2000	BAS, BSAS
GA	✓	✓		✓		SACS	0	10	1990	BAS, BS
HI	✓	✓	✓			WASC	1	1	2000	BAS
ID	✓	✓				NWCCU	0	3	1980	BAS, BAT
IL	✓	✓				NCA-HLC	0	11	1970	BS, BAAS
IN	✓	✓				NCA-HLC	0	3	1980	BA, BS
IA	✓	✓				NCA-HLC	0	3	2000	BAS
KS	✓	✓				NCA-HLC	0	3	2000	BAS, BAAS
KY	✓	✓				SACS	0	8	1990	BS, BA, BGS, BAGS, BALS
LA										
ME	✓	✓				NEASC	0	2	2000	BAS
MD										
MA										
MI	✓	✓				NCA-HLC	0	3	2000	BAS, BAA, BS

State	C1	C2	C3	C4	C5	C6	Accreditation			Year	Degrees
MN	✓	✓					NCA-HLC	0	7	1990	BAS
MS	✓	✓					SACS	0	1	2000	BAS
MO	✓	✓		✓			NCA-HLC	0	5	1970	BS, BSIT
MT	✓	✓					NWCCU	0	5	1990	BAS
NE	✓	✓					NCA-HLC	0	2	1980	BAS
NV	✓	✓					NWCCU	3	1	2000	BAS
NH	✓	✓	✓								
NJ					✓						
NM	✓	✓			✓		NCA-HLC	0	2	2000	BAS
NY	✓	✓					MSCHE	1	3	1970	BT, BBA
NC	✓	✓	✓				SACS	0	1	2000	BS, BSIT
ND	✓	✓	✓				NCA-HLC	1	3	2000	BAS
OH	✓	✓	✓				NCA-HLC	2	4	1990	BIS, BS, BAOT
OK	✓	✓	✓		✓		NCA-HLC	2	8	1980	BAAS, BAT, BT, BS
OR	✓	✓	✓		✓						
PA	✓						MSCHE	0	1	1980	BS
RI	✓	✓									
SC	✓	✓					SACS	0	3	2000	BS, BETM
SD	✓	✓					NCA-HLC	0	2	1990	BATS
TN	✓	✓					SACS	0	1	2000	BAS
TX	✓	✓	✓		✓		SACS	3	15	1980	BAT, BAAS
UT	✓	✓	✓				NWCCU	0	3	1990	BIS
VT	✓	✓	✓				NEASC	0	1	1980	BS
VA	✓				✓						
WA	✓	✓					NWCCU	4	4	2000	BAS
WV	✓	✓	✓				NCA-HLC	1	4	2000	BAS, BAT
WI	✓	✓	✓				NCA-HLC	0	2	2000	BAS
WY	✓	✓					NCA-HLC	0	1	2000	BAS

states would move toward transfer options for these associate's degree hold-ers. Employers also wanted paths of transfer for their employees with applied associate's degrees who could not advance in their careers without a baccalau-reate degree. In our conversations with students during our second phase of research, we found that many applied associate degree graduates had been told by other four-year institutions that, in order to obtain a baccalaureate degree, they would have to start over or transfer a limited number of credits. This approach produces an inefficient system for students who are looking to advance in their careers and who want additional technical or managerial training to supplement their associate's degrees.

Related to the factor of enhancing transfer for technical associate's degree holders is the factor of assisting adult learners in their completion of baccalaureate degrees. The population of adults is an often overlooked population, especially those who bring limited educational background but substantial experience in the workforce. To respond, many states and institu-tions developed AB degrees with adults in mind. Most AB programs offered across the nation feature adult-tailored approaches, such as online and dis-tance education options, night and weekend course work, and integration of policies that apply workforce and prior experience as credit. The latter of these options, credit-for-experience, is an option that is gaining momentum nationally (Klein-Collins, 2010), as states look for ways to facilitate adults toward degree attainment. Adults are also a primary target group for college completion degree programs. An example is in Kentucky, mentioned pre-viously for their requirement of all public four-year institutions to award completion degrees that can apply any associate's degree toward a baccalaure-ate. These degrees were created specifically for adults; according to state officials, there are many in the state with considerable credit but no creden-tial. Particularly of interest to those offering completion degrees are the "low-hanging fruit," those individuals who only need 20–30 additional credits for a baccalaureate degree. To some, these types of completion degrees are considered AB degrees due to their full incorporation of applied associate's degrees toward baccalaureate transfer.

AB degrees did not come without opposition to their implementation. Probably the most common responses to AB degrees in states that had not adopted such degrees were questions about rigor and quality. Officials in several states, including Mississippi and Iowa, noted that institutional administrators, particularly those in baccalaureate degree–granting institu-tions, expressed concern over AB degrees, because they might not be "per-ceived as being as rigorous as traditional baccalaureate programs" and involved a large number of technical credits such that rigor was brought into question. Because most AB programs have a large general education component to comply with state and accreditation guidelines, their acceptance of two entire years of 100- and 200-level course work in addition to general education courses leaves little room for upper-division courses.

Additionally, several officials in states that did not offer AB degrees posed that many alternatives were offered to the AB, which reduced demand for such degrees. An example is the use of university centers (also known as higher education centers), wherein four-year institutions offer baccalaureate-level programs at community colleges or other areas with little geographic access to baccalaureate education. These often include strong articulation agreements between two- and four-year institutions, so students who enter associate's degree programs can be assured of a baccalaureate degree pathway. Some of our interviewees observed that this does little to facilitate completion for those with applied associate's degrees and adults with some college credit but no degree, because it emphasizes the traditional pathway to the baccalaureate degree.

Phase Two Research

At the conclusion of the first phase, researchers identified several key features of AB degrees that merited closer attention. As a result, the second phase of research featured case studies of six states with unique approaches to AB degrees. These six states were chosen for several reasons. The first reason is for their ability to serve as representative models for other states. Some states would not have been adequate models, either because their approach to AB degrees was atypical, their governance structure was unlike that in other states, or it did not seem as if the state's method for implementing and maintaining AB degrees would be applicable to other states. The second reason is for having unique approaches. Whereas one state (such as Kentucky) approached the AB degree via providing completion degrees that would incorporate all associate's degrees, including applied associate's degrees, another state (such as Texas) allowed for the development of AB degrees at both two- and four-year institutions and fitting a number of unique AB curricular models. The third reason for choosing states was for having a broad scope and notable enrollments. Some states that seemed to have interesting approaches simply did not have high enrollments in AB degree programs, or were considering the possibility of discontinuing these programs, and were therefore not considered viable options for the case studies.

The six states chosen were Arizona, Florida, Kentucky, Oklahoma, Texas, and Washington. Arizona was chosen because it represented a decentralized governance structure but had in place a statewide AB articulation committee that focused on issues related to AB degrees. Such degrees have good support in the state, and their delivery models often include distance and online educational opportunities, owing to the geography of the state and the vast amount of rural area. Florida was chosen because they had a well-established community college baccalaureate (CCB) system in place that includes AB degrees. Florida is recognized by many as a model state for CCB implementation, and enrollments in the state's AB degree programs are high. Kentucky, as mentioned earlier, is notable for their curricular approach, through the mandatory creation of baccalaureate completion degrees in all four-year public institutions that are required to allow for full transfer of applied associate degrees. Kentucky is also recognized as a national leader in policies that address adult learners, a primary population in our study.

Oklahoma was chosen as a state with the AB degree offered at both two-year and four-year institutions; the two-year institutions that provide AB degrees are branch campuses of the larger Oklahoma State University system. They also provide a large number of AB degrees across the state in public four-year institutions that also provide associate's degrees, a unique institutional type that is in several states across the United States. Texas was chosen because they have the most four-year institutions that provide AB degrees of any state in the country. Enrollments are relatively high in several of these institutions as well. Texas also has, in limited numbers, the community college AB degree. Finally, Washington was chosen as a representative model of AB degree development within the past five years, as through legislation passed in the mid- to late-2000s they began to expand AB degrees as part of a statewide effort and began to allow community colleges to award AB degrees.

Once the six states were chosen by the researchers and the advisory group, a case study protocol was developed. Researchers visited state higher education governance offices and institutions that provide AB degrees to conduct interviews with a number of different individuals: state academic officers and higher education administrators, institutional administrators, institutional support staff, faculty, and students. Interview protocols were developed for each interview population. In addition to conducting interviews, research staff also started collection of enrollment data, when available.

Interview protocols aimed to collect a variety of data. The first goal of the case study visits was to verify and expand the current understandings of each of the states. Although we already had a sense of the extent to which AB degrees were offered in each of the six states, verifying the inventory data turned out to be important, because some states had had new developments since the 2007–2008 inventory. For example, Washington State had passed legislation allowing AB degrees to be offered at more community colleges, and specifically required that at least one AB program should be offered at a two-year technical college. In addition to verifying and expanding inventory data, our interview protocols aimed to document the perspectives of stakeholders in regard to AB degrees within the state. By interviewing individuals from several perspectives (state level, institutional level, faculty, and students), we were able to see how these degrees are viewed by different populations.

Once data were collected, and at the conclusion of the project in February 2011, they were compiled and analyzed for patterns, both within and between states, to recognize unique perspectives and approaches made by states as well as those that seemed to be common among several or all of our case study states. These results were compared with preliminary quantitative data to see how the strength of program enrollment compared with curricular models, degree fields, and other areas, to see which seemed most promising.

Phase Two Results

One of the most important reasons we conducted the second phase of research was to gather the myriad perspectives of stakeholders on these degrees. Although we gained a sense during the first phase of research of the perspective of state-level officials, we typically only interviewed one individual at the state level. In state offices during second phase research, we were able to determine how AB degrees played into the larger scheme of the state agenda for higher education. For example, in Oklahoma, we were able to interview individuals from the statewide Board of Regents' offices of Academic Affairs, Educational Partnerships, GEAR UP, Workforce Development, and state offices, including the Department of Commerce as well as the Governor's Council on Workforce and Economic Development. This gave us a good idea of how well-aware individuals in different offices were regarding AB degrees. All of the individuals we spoke with knew enough about AB degrees to answer some general questions, and in Oklahoma, where most of the AB degrees were management capstones or technical programs, the impact of AB degrees on the workforce was notable. It appeared that these degrees had the broad support of administrators and officials from a variety of offices, who seemed to view the degrees as providing equitable education to adults and those in the workforce, and providing highly specialized training in high-growth fields, particularly STEM fields.

Institutional administrators also tended to have favorable opinions of AB degrees in the six states we visited. For most institutions visited, we were able to talk with upper-level administrators, like presidents, vice presidents, and chief academic officers; mid-level administrators, such as deans, department heads, and support services directors; as well as professors and instructors in the specific programs. By far the staff members most supportive of AB degrees were the instructors and department heads, as they typically had participated in the development and maintenance of the AB degrees. In Arizona, for example, instructors, student support administrators, and program deans at Arizona State University–Polytechnic and Arizona State University–West were largely supportive of their AB programs. Advisors in the various departments were able to see firsthand how well received such programs were and how AB programs like those in emergency services administration would aid current emergency services employees who wanted to work full time and still finish a baccalaureate degree. Instructors even went so far as to say that many students in the various programs would not have had much of a chance of completing or even starting a baccalaureate program had the AB degrees not been implemented. This was especially true of those programs that specifically targeted adult students, where innovative policies and practices were instrumental in creating reachable pathways to the baccalaureate.

The six states chosen proved to be instrumental in providing many models of approaches to the provision of AB degrees. One of the first things noted in data analysis was the difference in issues states faced based on whether they awarded the AB degree at the two- and four-year institutional level or at the four-year level only. Florida, Texas, and Washington, who all had policies in place to allow community colleges to award AB degrees, all had to follow very specific procedures in order to begin awarding these degrees. The first was accreditation. According to state and institutional officials, the shift from awarding degrees at no higher level than associate degrees to awarding baccalaureate degrees required special consideration from accreditors. Accreditors often look to institutional mission when making decisions regarding whether to accredit degree programs. Community colleges that have approval to award AB degrees from the state must be able to exhibit that baccalaureate degrees are consistent with their particular institutional mission. This issue was not nearly as difficult to approach for Oklahoma, which does have two two-year institutions that award ABs. The reason stems from these two institutions being branch campuses of the Oklahoma State University system. The system had already been authorized to award four-year baccalaureate degrees, even AB degrees; for these two institutions, they needed to receive approval from the OSU system, as well as program approval from the Oklahoma State's Board of Regents. This process, although still difficult, is not nearly as involved as the process of approving the AB degree at community colleges.

Another challenge to the AB degree awarded by two-year institutions comes typically from four-year institutions. One concern noted by officials in all of the two-year AB states was that administrators at the four-year institutions were worried about degree duplication, which would be inefficient and create unnecessary competition, as well as require additional state funding to provide the degrees from multiple institutions. Because community colleges are often within the same geographic areas as competing four-year colleges and universities, this concern is understandable. States like Florida and Washington, with well-established community college baccalaureate policies, have addressed these concerns by limiting the degrees that two-year institutions can award. Washington has made it clear in legislation that programs must be approved by the State Board and must fall into several categories, such as technical AB programs, or baccalaureate degrees in nursing. Community and technical colleges in these states do not have the flexibility to award any baccalaureate degrees they choose. This seems to be a reasonable compromise, but in Florida, some community colleges do offer baccalaureate degrees in fields such as education, where competition with four-year institutions could occur. In the case of Florida, community colleges were granted authority to award these degrees because of overcrowding in four-year institutions. To solve the capacity issues, state officials and lawmakers had to choose between spending additional funding to allow four-year institutions to expand their physical campuses to address the rise in enrollments, or to allow other institutions like community colleges to award degrees and alleviate the overcrowding issues in-state. Florida chose the latter, and although there is still some resistance to these policies, it appears that most of the community college baccalaureate degrees, including the AB degrees, are being sustained in the state.

All six states cited adult learners as a specific population addressed by AB degrees. This is an important finding, as many of the issues that pervade discussions on higher education and the value of baccalaureate education carry the implicit assumption of traditional baccalaureate degrees with traditional undergraduate students. For many adults, the purpose of education is not to gain a liberal education, or to explore career options. For these individuals, the career path has already been chosen, and the baccalaureate degree is seen as a means to continuing up the career ladder. Whereas more broadly general baccalaureate degrees allow graduates the opportunities to pursue a number of career fields, AB degrees are often designed with specific career pathways in mind. It is in their specificity that they are effective programs for adult learners.

There are traditional college-age students who participate in AB programs, even those that are highly specialized, but from our interviews, these students were often atypical in that they already knew precisely what career path they wanted to take. For example, Oklahoma State University Institute of Technology's bachelor of technology degree in information assurance and forensics, which is accredited by the Accreditation Board for Engineering and Technology, deals specifically with computer forensics and security, and is a highly specialized field. In our focus group interview with seven students in the program, we found that many of these students were of traditional college age, but were certain the field was where they wanted to go. Said one student during this interview, "they (the program staff) wanted to set you up with an employer, and they want to push you and get you working as soon as possible [after graduation]. That was one of the things that I wanted to do." Consequently, this specific program boasts a 100% employment placement rate following graduation, which has been used to assure students interested in pursuing the program that they will succeed when they graduate.

Discussion

The information and analyses from both phases of research contribute to the larger discussion regarding the definition and application of a baccalaureate education. Toward the end of our second phase of research, it became clear to us that many issues with AB development related to larger contextual

questions regarding educational quality, the definition of baccalaureate programs, the role of workforce education in contemporary higher education,
and others. We also wanted to receive additional viewpoints from those outside of specific states and institutions. As a result, in early September 2010,
Lumina Foundation for Education sponsored a convening on the AB, which
we led, along with Holly Zanville and other Lumina staff. Several groups of
individuals were invited to the discussion, including state-level administrators in higher education, researchers, institutional administrators, staff, and
faculty, as well as national experts and regional accrediting body presidents.
Approximately 100 individuals attended, representing a wide diversity of
viewpoints on higher education across the nation as well as in Canada.

At this convening, two different but distinctly related issues came to the
forefront of the discussion. The first was on the merits and debate surrounding the community college baccalaureate (CCB). The second was on the
value and meaning of a baccalaureate education. These issues are highly
interrelated, because the questions surrounding the quality and efficacy of
AB programs are often the same questions asked of CCB degrees. Whereas
most CCB degrees offered are AB degrees, there are many offered in traditional fields, such as teaching, liberal arts, and others. Similarly, there are AB
programs that are not offered in the community college; in fact, most AB
programs offered nationally are not at the community college level. It was
important to make that distinction in the discussions at that convening, but
both issues were discussed at length. (For more information specifically on
that convening, please refer to Ruud & Bragg, 2011.)

Baccalaureate Education

What seems clear regarding the course baccalaureate education will be taking
in the future is that it will be moving beyond simply the counting of credits.
Michael Boulus and Nathan Daun-Barnett's (2008) *A Defense of Baccalaureate Education* makes this assertion as well, but goes further to challenge the
AB degree for relying on credit counts to make up a baccalaureate degree. It
should be noted that the report comes out of Michigan, where state and
institutional administrators are currently embroiled in a debate over community college baccalaureate degrees, which include AB degrees at community
colleges. Because the AB degree has come to prominence in several states,
the answer to the question regarding the concise definition of a baccalaureate
degree becomes less clear. When applied degrees were considered terminal

and nontransferable, there was little concern for the outcomes of applied course work within the context of baccalaureate education. Now that credit associated with applied courses and degrees is being allowed to transfer, these courses are receiving greater scrutiny from numerous stakeholders, particularly accreditors, policy makers, and educators at the university level.

The strict requirements of general education will not disappear in light of AB degrees. Only in a handful of states are general education requirements *different* for AB degrees than for traditional baccalaureate degrees, and in these states, the differences are only by a few credits, and they still take into account accreditation and state-mandated general education minimum requirements. Because of these careful counts on general education courses, it is more difficult for educators to simply accept applied associate degrees as a block of transfer; instead, although the block might transfer, general education courses are audited, and students will be required to fulfill whatever deficits might be in place. Some states and institutions get around this by requiring the minimum general education requirements for the two years of the AB degree, rather than addressing whatever general education courses were obtained during the associate's degree. Because many applied associate's degrees require general education courses, this seems like a reasonable solution. However, this could result in students taking *too many* prerequisite courses and not being able to continue on to the upper-division course work desired by employers and students alike, or extending time to degree to satisfy the traditional general education and upper-division requirements, thus extending and possibly jeopardizing completion.

Another important consideration to make regards the differences that AB degree models take. Building on the work of Ignash and Kotun (2005), our work has largely posited the existence of four distinct AB curricular models: The upside-down degree model, which takes a wide variety of applied associate's degrees and applies the general education and elective credits required to fulfill credit requirements; the management model, which takes a somewhat limited number of applied associate's degrees and adds a management or business capstone, which is helpful for those looking to enter mid-level management in their careers; career ladder models, which apply a significant portion of additional technical course work on an already technically oriented applied associate degree; and a hybrid model, which incorporates aspects of two or three of the curricular models. With the exception of programs in Kentucky, the majority of AB programs examined by second phase research fit into career ladder, management, or hybridized models, emphasizing technical and business-related course work to enhance career upward mobility for graduates.

Because of these different models, it is difficult to generalize AB degrees within a certain context of baccalaureate education. This is especially true for those degrees designated as upside-down versus those that apply management or technical course work. Completion degrees are not designed specifically for applied associate's degrees; instead, they are designed to accept credits from virtually any source and apply whatever credits are necessary to meet baccalaureate degree requirements. Because of this, questions about the rigor of such programs differ from those that incorporate specialized course plans that lead to AB degrees that fit the other curricular models. In other words, AB degree curricular models can vary in the extent to which they offer specialization, which can make them fit into a wide variety of baccalau reate degree types.

Those interested in the AB degree, particularly within the context of the defining of baccalaureate education, should look into the philosophical and practical questions surrounding the purpose of baccalaureate education. At the root, one could argue that all degrees awarded by baccalaureate-granting institutions are "workforce" degrees; some may be more technical and others are more liberal, but all are awarded ultimately to lead to employment. The real issue is that technical course work may be seen as of lower quality, whereas liberal education as more academic and therefore more rigorous. However, does a liberal education constitute more rigorous education? Our findings indicate AB degrees are more nuanced than these simplistic debates suggest, and questions of rigor and quality are more subjective than most would prefer. In basic terms, the variety of AB curricular models makes them impossible to group into a single classification. Nearly all programs require the minimum general education requirements laid out by accreditors and state governments, so general education requirements are being met, but does meeting this requirement ensure rigor and quality? We contend matters of rigor and quality have as much to do with the content being taught and the pedagogical methods being used as the form of knowledge (e.g., technical versus liberal) being conveyed.

The question comes down to whether applied courses offered at the lower division prepare students for the upper division, and in some cases qualify for the awarding of upper-division credit. Instead of looking at credit counts and syllabi, we argue the advent of the AB degree shifts the conversation to where it needs to be—on student outcomes. What are we looking for from graduates of bachelor's degree programs? Can these outcomes be met by AB degrees? Although our academic approach to AB degrees keeps us from making a value judgment in regard to these questions, we have been able to see from our inventory and follow-up case studies that AB degree programs have wide support from stakeholders, including state and institutional administrators, faculty, employers, and students. To many, AB degrees fulfill a long-standing need for a better-educated workforce and facilitate baccalaureate completion for a population that has been awarded a historically terminal degree. If educational and vocational outcomes are being met by these degrees, it would suggest their feasibility as a facet within American higher education.

References

Boulus, M., & Daun-Barnett, N. (2008, May). *A defense of baccalaureate education.* Retrieved from http://www.pcsum.org/Portals/0/docs/Defense%20of%20Baccalaureate%20Education%20-%20FINAL.pdf

Bragg, D. D., Townsend, B. K., & Ruud, C. M. (2009, January). *The adult learner and the applied baccalaureate: Emerging lessons for state and local implementation.* Champaign: University of Illinois, Office of Community College Research and Leadership. Retrieved from http://occrl.illinois.edu/sites/occrl.illinois.edu/files/InBrief/AppBaccBrief.pdf

Cherry Commission. (2004). *Final report of the Lt. Governor's Commission on Higher Education & Economic Growth.* Retrieved from http://www.cherrycommission.org/docs/finalReport/CherryReportFULL.pdf

Chronicle of Higher Education. (2010). *The Chronicle almanac 2009–2010.* Retrieved from http://chronicle.com/section/Almanac-of-Higher-Education/141/

Floyd, D. L., Skolnik, M. L., & Walker, K. P. (Eds.). (2005). *Community college baccalaureate: Emerging trends and policy issues.* Sterling, VA: Stylus.

Floyd, D. L., & Walker, K. P. (2009). The community college baccalaureate: Putting the pieces together. *Community College Journal of Research and Practice, 33,* 90–124.

Ignash, J. M., & Kotun, D. (2005). Results of a national study of transfer in occupational/technical degrees: Policies and practices. *The Journal of Applied Research in the Community College, 12*(2), 109–120.

Klein-Collins, R. (2010). *Fueling the race to postsecondary success: A 48-institution study of prior learning assessment and adult student outcomes.* Chicago: The Council for Adult & Experiential Learning. Retrieved from http://www.cael.org/pdf/PLA_Fueling-the-Race.pdf

Levin, J. S. (2007). *Nontraditional students and community colleges: The conflict of justice and neoliberalism.* New York, NY: Palgrave Macmillan.

National Center for Education Statistics. (2009). *Digest of education statistics, 2008* (NCES 2009-020). Washington, DC: National Center for Education Statistics.

Osborne, M., Marks., A., & Turner, E. (2004). Becoming a mature student: How adult applicants weigh the advantages and disadvantages of higher education. *Higher Education, 48,* 291–315.

Ruud, C. M., & Bragg, D. D. (2011). *The applied baccalaureate: What we know, what we learned, and what we need to know.* Champaign: Office of Community College Research and Leadership, University of Illinois at Urbana-Champaign.

Scoheff, M., Jr. (2009, July 14). Obama, private sector call for better workforce preparation. *Workforce Management.* Retrieved from http://www.workforce.com/section/news/article/obama-private-sector-call-better-workforce-preparation.php

Townsend, B. K., Bragg, D. D., & Ruud, C. M. (2008). *The adult learner and the applied baccalaureate: National and state-by-state inventory.* Retrieved from http://education.missouri.edu/orgs/cccr/_files/Final%20Inventory.pdf

9

REFLECTIONS ON THE NATURE AND STATUS OF THE APPLIED BACCALAUREATE DEGREE

Drawing Upon the Canadian Experience

Michael L. Skolnik

B accalaureate degrees awarded by community colleges are predominantly in applied areas of study and are designed to prepare graduates for specific occupations. These baccalaureate programs generally employ experiential learning methods such as learning-by-doing, and many programs include periods of paid work experience. Because of these characteristics, the degrees are often referred to as workforce baccalaureate degrees or, by the term that will be used in this chapter, *applied baccalaureate degrees.*

The emergence and recent growth in the number of applied baccalaureate degrees awarded by North American community colleges have given rise to questions concerning the meaning of these new degrees, how they compare with traditional academic baccalaureate degrees awarded by four-year institutions, and the status of baccalaureate degrees awarded by community colleges. Drawing upon the experience of Canadian community colleges with applied baccalaureate programs, this chapter explores these questions. The chapter begins with a description of the origins, prevalence, and current state of the applied baccalaureate degree in Canada's community colleges. In the first section of the chapter it is noted that although the regulations that enable community colleges to award baccalaureate degrees restrict their baccalaureate-granting authority to applied baccalaureate degrees, the regulations contain little or nothing in the way of defining what an applied baccalaureate degree is. The first section also notes some differences in scale and terminology between Canada and the United States regarding the community college baccalaureate. The next and main section of the chapter examines the concept of an applied baccalaureate, describes how the concept has been operationalized in practice, and explores questions about the nature and status of the degree. Following this discussion, the chapter ends with some brief concluding comments.

The Development and State of the Community College Baccalaureate in Canada

Community colleges in Canada began offering their own baccalaureate programs in the early 1990s. As of February 2011, 32 community colleges in Canada were offering 141 baccalaureate programs.[1] This number of baccalaureate programs offered by community colleges now is substantially lower than a few years ago, because it excludes the programs of six former community colleges and university-colleges that recently have been converted into universities.[2] With or without the inclusion of these six institutions, the scale of the community college baccalaureate relative to population and to the total number of community colleges is much greater in Canada than in the United States. Alene Russell reported that 54 community colleges in the United States were offering 465 baccalaureate programs (Russell, 2010). Thus, with about 10 times the population and number of community colleges in the United States, there are fewer than twice as many colleges that offer baccalaureate programs, and the number of such programs in the United States is only a little more than three times as great as in Canada.

Although the organization of higher education and the role of community colleges are broadly similar in Canada and the United States, there are a few differences in both practices and conventional terminology. Traditionally the word *university* has been used in Canada to refer to a postsecondary institution that has statutory authority to award the baccalaureate or the baccalaureate and higher degrees, and for which the majority of its academic awards are at the level of the baccalaureate or higher. The term *college*, without a modifier, has been used to refer to community colleges and technical institutes. Collectively, the members of the Association of Canadian Community Colleges are commonly referred to as "colleges and institutes." In regard to academic awards, these institutions traditionally have concentrated on certificates and diplomas. The associate's degree has been awarded in only one province, British Columbia. The terms *two-year* and *four-year institutions* have not been used in Canada and would not be appropriate, because some community colleges offer three-year programs, and many universities have offered, and a number still offer, three-year baccalaureate degrees.

Presently community colleges have the authority to award baccalaureate degrees, subject to ministerial approval on a program-by-program basis, in 5 of Canada's 10 provinces. In 3 of Canada's 4 largest provinces—Alberta, British Columbia, and Ontario—colleges have been awarding a substantial number of baccalaureate degrees for several years. In Manitoba, the bill that enables colleges to award "baccalaureate degrees with an applied focus" was enacted in June 2009, and in Prince Edward Island, the province's only college has thus far obtained approval to award only a single "applied degree," in culinary operations.

The author has previously related the beginnings of the community college baccalaureate in Canada (Skolnik, 2005), and it will be summarized only briefly here. The idea of colleges awarding baccalaureate degrees first surfaced in British Columbia in the late 1980s. Out of concern that British Columbia was near the bottom among Canada's provinces in baccalaureate completion and enrollment rates, the government established a committee on postsecondary access. The committee noted that the universities were concentrated in the most populous parts of the province and recommended allowing some of the colleges in more distant parts of the province to add third and fourth years of undergraduate studies (Provincial Access Committee, 1988; see also Dennison, 1997). Three colleges that were far from the two largest cities, which housed the universities, were given the authority to add third and fourth years and were renamed "university-colleges," reflecting their dual functions as universities and as colleges. Subsequently, it was recognized that to achieve a substantial increase in the number of students completing the baccalaureate in the province would require an expansion of opportunity for baccalaureate study in or near the major cities, because that was where so much of the population resided. Accordingly, a fourth college, on the outskirts of the Vancouver metropolitan area, was made into a university-college, and then a fifth university-college even closer to Vancouver was approved. Political pressure from the Vancouver region also contributed to the decision to let that region have university-colleges, too. Perhaps reflecting the fact that the same distance-related access issue that justified the first three university-colleges did not exist in the case of the fifth university-college, its authority to award baccalaureate degrees was restricted to "applied" degrees. Thus, what started from an *access* rationale to give students in more distant regions of the province the opportunity to do the same kinds of baccalaureate degrees as residents in the most populous regions had was extended to the idea of community colleges offering a new kind of baccalaureate degree that was somehow different from the traditional baccalaureate program that the universities, and the first university-colleges, had been offering. However, complicating this extension of the concept of the community college baccalaureate, the government failed to define the term *applied* despite urging by the colleges that it do so (Carr, 2001).

Once one of the university-colleges started offering applied baccalaureate degrees, it was not long before the government had to allow all of the community colleges to award applied baccalaureate degrees. By 2008, all but one of the university-colleges had become universities, and the other one became a campus of the University of British Columbia. Now all the community colleges in the province are eligible to award applied—and only applied—baccalaureate degrees.

In contrast to British Columbia where the original rationale for allowing colleges to award the baccalaureate degree was to improve access, in Alberta the community college baccalaureate was "designed in response to employer demand in emerging occupations" (Campus Alberta Quality Council, 2010, p. 68). The government believed that there was a need for workers with similar but more advanced workforce preparation than what graduates of two-year diploma programs in the colleges were receiving. The solution was to extend the existing diplomas by adding an additional two semesters of classroom study and add two semesters of "directed field study." Although the new degrees all had the word *bachelor* (as well as the word *applied*) in their formal names, in government documents they were referred to simply as "applied degrees" rather than as applied *baccalaureate* degrees. On their websites, Alberta colleges often refer to their applied degree programs as "two-year" programs, because they normally require two years for an applicant who has completed a two-year diploma in the related career program in an Alberta college to complete.

From the outset, the government indicated that the applied degrees were to be considered "terminal," and that graduates should not expect to be admitted to master's programs and other university programs that normally required an undergraduate degree for admission (Government of Alberta, 2011). Although graduates of the applied degree programs face uncertain prospects regarding further education, anecdotal reports indicate that some have been admitted to master of business administration programs and other university programs that require an undergraduate degree, and there are some agreements between Alberta colleges and universities in Canada to facilitate such transitions. A recent government survey showed that 0.9% of applied degree graduates entered a graduate program within four years of graduation, compared with 7.3% for conventional baccalaureate graduates (Alberta Advanced Education and Technology, 2011). The survey also noted that applied degree graduates are only one-tenth as likely to apply for graduate study as are graduates of conventional baccalaureate programs. Two other noteworthy findings of the survey were: Applied degree graduates were more satisfied with their educational experience than graduates of other types of postsecondary programs; and the median salary of applied degree graduates was 8.7% higher than that of other baccalaureate graduates, and 28.2% higher than that of diploma graduates. The survey report concluded that the "applied degrees are meeting the needs of the specific employment markets as originally intended" (Alberta Advanced Education and Technology, 2011, p. 2).

The applied degree programs in Alberta were introduced in 1995–1996, and until 2004 proposals for these programs were reviewed only by the Ministry of Advanced Education and Career Development. Colleges had to show that there was a demand for graduates of an applied degree program beyond that for the related diploma program and that employers supported the work experience component of the program. By 2003, 27 programs had been approved at 9 of the province's 16 colleges and both institutes of technology. Programs were in such fields as petroleum engineering technology and applied information services technology.

There have been two significant developments regarding the community college baccalaureate in Alberta since 2004. The first pertains to the approval process for applied degree programs. In 2004 proposals for new applied degree programs became subject to review by a new postsecondary education agency, the Campus Alberta Quality Council. The CAQC was given the responsibility for review of all proposed new degree programs of the universities and colleges. Perusal of the annual reports of the CAQC shows that there have been applications for only two new applied degree programs, both from the same college, since the responsibility for review of such programs was given to the CAQC in 2004. This observation stands somewhat in contrast to the 2011 survey report referred to earlier that concluded that the applied degrees were meeting the needs for which they were intended.

The second development helps to explain why there have been so few new applications for applied degree programs since 2004. The two colleges that offered the largest numbers of applied degree programs, Mount Royal

College in Calgary and Grant MacEwan College in Edmonton, were given the authority to offer "academic" baccalaureate programs in addition to their applied degree programs and their traditional community college programs. In 2007, the mission of these institutions was formally changed from that of community colleges to the province's two "baccalaureate granting colleges" (Alberta Ministry of Advanced Education and Career Development, 2007). In 2009, both institutions became universities. After becoming eligible to offer conventional baccalaureate programs in 2007, both institutions ceased developing new applied degree programs and began converting their applied degree programs to academic baccalaureate programs. Similarly, after the two institutes of technology, which also are in Calgary and Edmonton, were designated as polytechnic institutions and given the authority to award academic baccalaureate degrees, they both ceased submitting proposals for new applied degree programs.

The provincial government's decision to allow these four institutions in the two largest cities that have accounted for the largest numbers of applied degree programs in Alberta colleges to award academic baccalaureates is a large part of the explanation for the near absence of new proposals for applied degree programs in recent years. New proposals for baccalaureate programs from these institutions have been only for academic baccalaureate programs. However, this does not explain why so few proposals for new applied degree programs have been submitted by the other colleges. One possible reason for the dearth of new applied degree program proposals from these colleges since 2004 is that the approval process for applied degrees might be perceived as more arduous and uncertain since the establishment of the CAQC, whose purview consists almost entirely of conventional university programs, and most of whose members have a conventional university background. Moreover, the two-year diploma is an integral component of the applied degree, but assessing the diplomas is not within the mandate of the CAQC. The fact that the CAQC has no experience with assessing what is actually about two-thirds of the curriculum content of applied degree programs could fuel the feeling of some college educators that people from the universities do not understand the applied degree, and hence could not render sound judgments on proposals for new applied degrees. On the other hand, the decline in the number of new proposals may simply be owing to diminished prestige of the applied degree, resulting from the shift of interest away from that degree by the largest college sector institutions in the largest cities.

When Ontario's colleges were given the opportunity to award baccalaureate degrees in applied fields of study in 2000, the government indicated that the rationale for this move was both to expand access to the baccalaureate and to provide industry a supply of graduates with a new, more applied, type of career preparation. It is likely that another factor in the government's decision to allow the colleges to award baccalaureate degrees was its inability to get the province's universities to be more accommodating in regard to transfer arrangements for graduates of diploma programs in the colleges who wished to pursue a baccalaureate degree in a university (Skolnik, 2009). Since the colleges were first allowed to submit proposals for baccalaureate programs after the year 2000 legislation, there has been a steady increase in the number of such programs offered by the colleges. However, there has also been a move toward concentration of these programs in a relatively small number of colleges. As of February 2011, four institutions accounted for 71% of the baccalaureate programs offered by Ontario's colleges (derived from data on the website of the Postsecondary Education Quality Assessment Board, 2011). Twelve of the system's 24 colleges were continuing to offer baccalaureate programs, after some that had originally obtained approval to offer at least one baccalaureate program withdrew from offering baccalaureate programs or were phasing out their programs.

The Concept of the Applied Baccalaureate Degree and Its Application in Canada

Although the term *applied* is frequently used in conjunction with baccalaureate programs offered by community colleges, the term is rarely defined and often used in different ways. Moreover, the term *applied* is sometimes used to refer to baccalaureate programs developed by universities to accommodate students transferring from career programs in community colleges.

In the Adult Learner and the Applied Baccalaureate study, funded by the Lumina Foundation for Education, Barbara Townsend, Debra Bragg, and Collin Ruud (2008) defined the *applied baccalaureate* as "a bachelor's degree designed to incorporate applied associate courses and degrees once considered as 'terminal' or non-baccalaureate level while providing students with the higher-order thinking skills and advanced technical knowledge and skills so desired in today's job market" (Townsend, Bragg, & Ruud, 2008, p. iv). Under this definition, the applied baccalaureate experience must include a particular type of program (applied associate degree) in a particular type of institution (community college) for the first two years. The remainder of the curriculum may be provided either by a traditional baccalaureate-granting institution through transfer from a community college, or by a community college offering the complete baccalaureate program. In this definition, the focus of the applied baccalaureate is on facilitating baccalaureate completion for students in applied associate's degree programs.

The applied baccalaureate degree in Canada that fits the Townsend, Bragg, and Ruud definition most closely is the Alberta applied degree. These are the only baccalaureate programs in Canada that are defined with reference to prior diploma programs. As noted earlier, the applied degree was originally developed to consist of the two-year diploma curriculum plus one additional year of classroom study and one year of directed field study.[3]

Probably the most obvious way of conceptualizing the term *applied* is in regard to field of study. For example, the legislation in Ontario gives colleges the authority to award degrees in "applied fields of study." However, the legislation does not give any guidance as to what is or is not an applied field of study. Presumably, police studies or early childhood education would be applied fields, whereas political studies or geography would not be applied fields. However, one can imagine programs in the first two fields whose focus would not be training practitioners and programs in the latter two fields whose orientation would be toward practice. As Sheldon Rothblatt notes, "there is no subject that cannot be taught illiberally, no subject that cannot be taught liberally" (Rothblatt, 1993, p. 64). Insofar as this observation is valid, one needs to look at the goals of a program and how learning is facilitated in order to determine whether it involves applied study.

Baccalaureate programs in Canadian community colleges often emphasize the integration of theory and practice and require periods of supervised work experience. However, beyond references to these characteristics of the programs, there is not much detail about curriculum or pedagogy in applied baccalaureate programs in the handbooks of the relevant provincial agencies in Alberta, British Columbia, or Ontario. For example, the British Columbia document on degree program approval criteria and guidelines provides the following description of "programs with an applied focus":

> They blend theory and practice, with content selected to ensure mastery of the field of practice, and prepare students for employment and for advanced study in relevant graduate and professional programs. (British Columbia Ministry of Advanced Education, 2008, p. 16)

A more elaborated discussion of the applied nature of career-focused community college programs and how these programs differ from typical university programs, even in related fields of study, has been provided by Gilles Paquet (2006) in a background paper prepared for a review of postsecondary education in British Columbia. Paquet does not refer specifically to baccalaureate programs in the colleges, but to the general orientation of the colleges that might be assumed to permeate their baccalaureate as well as their other programs. Paquet focuses on the goals and functions of postsecondary education, and he argues that Canadian postsecondary education suffers from a truncation between the development of the mind and the ability to reason, on the one hand, and the acquisition of skills and practical knowledge, on the other. He argues that in general, the tendency of the universities is to concentrate on the former, and of the colleges is to concentrate on the latter, although one can find examples of each function in both sectors. In Paquet's formulation, the applied orientation of the colleges relates to the primary goal that the institutions set for themselves: imparting "knowledge that is practical, instrumental, product-oriented know-how" (p. 19). This stands in contrast to the universities' emphasis on "knowledge that is universal, general, and non-contextual" (p. 19). Paquet goes on to say that knowledge in the university has become construed more and more in terms of the development of the capability to analyze and reason through content-neutral curricula and emphasis on theory and especially on methodology, and a corresponding lessening or abandoning interest in the local, particular, and contextual.

These two major functions of postsecondary education are not perceived as being of equal status. The institutions that concentrate mostly on the development of analysis and reasoning capabilities occupy the highest rung of the postsecondary ladder. Institutions whose programs are judged to be more practical and skill-development-oriented as opposed to being more abstract and concept-oriented occupy a lower place on the status hierarchy, regardless of the sophistication and complexity of their curricula. Paquet laments the separation of these two functions of postsecondary education into distinct spheres and institutions. He maintains that integration of the two functions leads to more effective learning, personal and professional development, and better development of both the mind and of practical knowledge and skills.

If we try to turn from the goals of applied baccalaureate programs to the pedagogy employed in the programs, we discover that little has been written about the pedagogy used in such programs in Canada or the United States or even more generally, about pedagogy in community college career education programs at any level. Some authors have commented on the emphasis on "hands-on" or experiential learning in college programs, including baccalaureate programs, but these observations tend to be based on personal experience rather than on actual empirical research. For example, after noting the paucity of research on the pedagogies employed in career education (Achtenhagen & Grubb, 1999), Grubb and Associates observe that "legions of vocational teachers have asserted the virtue of 'hands-on' instruction" through such activities as working on engines, baking cakes, or constructing houses (Grubb & Associates, 1999, p. 106). In a related vein, Kenneth Walker and Deborah Floyd commented that applied baccalaureates "differ from traditional baccalaureates in that they make considerable use of 'applied' and contextual learning methods, and significant learning on the job while traditional baccalaureates depend principally on academic pedagogy" (Walker & Floyd, 2005, p. 96). Besides the terms *hands-on* and *experiential*, another term that has been used to elaborate on the notion of applied learning is *inductive learning*. Charles Pascal, a professor of human development and applied psychology in the University of Toronto, and a former college president and chair of the agency that used to oversee the college system in Ontario, observed that colleges have often been described as institutions that tend to give greater emphasis to inductive learning in contrast to universities where deductive learning is more prominent (Pascal, personal communication, May 9, 2011).

One of the most eloquent descriptions of inductive learning is the one provided by the 19th century philosopher Arthur Schopenhauer.[4] Schopenhauer suggested that the human intellect is "so constituted that *general ideas* arise by abstraction from particular observations" (Schopenhauer, 2005, p. 51). Forming general ideas from particular observations could be described as inductive learning and is what Schopenhauer called "the natural method of education." Schopenhauer believed that when a person learns in this way, he "knows quite well which of his particular observations belong to and are represented by each of his general ideas" (Schopenhauer, 2005, p. 51).

Schopenhauer contrasted this method of learning with what he called the *artificial* method of learning. The artificial method is to acquire general ideas from listening to other people and from reading before one has any sort of "extended acquaintance with the world as it is, and as you may see it for yourself" (Schopenhauer, 2005, p. 51). In this method, the learner may be told that the particular observations that go into making the general ideas will come later in the course of experience. The philosopher argued that without one's own firsthand experience of these observations, there is a good chance that one will apply the general ideas incorrectly and judge people and things from a wrong standpoint. Schopenhauer applied this distinction between ways of learning to the education of children. He maintained that what he called the artificial method should not be used at too young an age, lest:

> Instead of developing the child's own faculties of discernment, and teaching it to judge and think for itself, the teacher uses all his energies to stuff its head full of the ready-made thoughts of other people. The mistaken views of life, which spring from a false application of general ideas, have afterwards to be corrected by long years of experience; and it is seldom that they are wholly corrected. This is why so few men of learning are possessed of common-sense, such as is often to be met with in people who have had no instruction at all. (Schopenhauer, 2005, p. 52)

Schopenhauer urged that no idea should ever be established in a child's mind otherwise than by what the child can see for itself, and suggested that the result of this would be that the child's ideas, even if few, would be well-grounded and accurate. The child would learn how to measure things by his or her own standard.

Although Schopenhauer's essay on education is concerned with the education of children, the same kind of choice that he depicted between different approaches to education, or ways of learning, exists for adolescents and adults. It may well be that what Schopenhauer called the natural method of education is more effective for certain fields of study, for example, the career fields in which colleges offer programs; or for certain individuals.

The notion that different learning styles are more effective with some individuals than with others has become a staple in research on learning in postsecondary education. Perhaps the most widely cited typology of learning styles, the one developed by David Kolb (1984), differentiates among learning styles on the basis of learners' comfort with such activities as doing and thinking, a distinction that has similarity to the one employed by Schopenhauer. Some of the research on learning styles in practice has shown systematic differences in preferred learning styles among practitioners in different career fields (Donohue, 2010). To the best of the author's knowledge, there have been no studies of learning styles that compared community college students with university students, but it is possible that there may be differences between these two sectors in regard to the comfort level of the majority of students with active experimentation relative to abstract conceptualization. If so, that would provide a reason for colleges to place greater emphasis than universities on applied learning. Of course even if there are differences between sectors in the preferred learning styles of the *majority* of students, there is likely to be variation in preferred learning styles within each sector. That variation would provide an argument for overlap of missions between colleges and universities in regard to the functions of postsecondary education.[5]

Although the applied nature of the educational experience that colleges provide may be a source of strength for their programs, it can also be their *Achilles heel.* Insofar as Paquet is correct about the higher status of a more theoretically framed approach to education, the applied nature of college programs leaves them open to the allegation that they offer second-class baccalaureate programs. It is probably for this reason that college educators in Ontario have tried to avoid referring to their baccalaureate programs as "applied baccalaureates." Rather, they make a point of using the phrase from the legislation, "baccalaureates in applied fields of study," when referring to their programs. The presidents of the colleges maintained that the term *applied* was "confusing to students and employers and has probably affected student interest in college [baccalaureate] degree programs" (Colleges Ontario, 2009, p. 5). After years of pressing the issue, in 2009, they got the government to drop the requirement that the word *applied* be in the formal title of an approved baccalaureate program. British Columbia has never had that requirement, and if one looked just at the titles of the baccalaureate programs offered by colleges in that province, one would be hard-pressed to guess whether they were college or university programs.

In summary, there appears to be something connoted by the term *applied*—that is not spelled out in much detail—that differentiates college baccalaureates in Ontario, and possibly also in British Columbia, from university baccalaureates, but at the same time the college baccalaureates are supposed to be of equivalent quality and meet the same standards as those of universities. Here is how the Ontario guidelines handle the dilemma of describing baccalaureate degrees that are intended to be different but not too different from academic baccalaureate degrees:

> A degree in an applied area of study is normally designed to require a level of conceptual sophistication, specialized knowledge and intellectual autonomy similar to that in an honours or specialist degree program but with the disciplinary content oriented to an occupational field of practice.

Students in applied programs learn by doing with a focus on preparing for entry into an occupational field of practice. Applied programs incorporate a blend of theory and practice . . . (Postsecondary Education Quality Assessment Board, 2010, p. 17)

The corresponding description of applied degrees in Alberta has some similarities with the British Columbia and Ontario statements. For example, the Campus Alberta Quality Council states that applied degrees "require a level of conceptual sophistication, specialized knowledge and intellectual autonomy similar to that of other baccalaureate programs . . ." (Campus Alberta Quality Council, 2010, p. 68). However, because the required curriculum structure of these programs is so different from that of the other baccalaureate programs, and perhaps because they are popularly referred to simply as applied degree programs, the applied degree programs in Alberta seem to be perceived differently than the academic baccalaureate programs. The best evidence of this difference in perceptions is that when any postsecondary institution in the province has acquired the authority to offer *both* academic and applied baccalaureate programs, from then on it has developed *only* academic baccalaureate programs. Thus, the experience with respect to the relationship between community college and university equivalent baccalaureate programs is different in Alberta than in Ontario or British Columbia.

It is possible that college educators have been overly sensitive about the word *applied*. After all, it is still common for engineering in Canadian universities to be offered in a faculty of *applied* science and engineering, or simply a faculty of *applied* science.[6] Nevertheless, because the prefix *applied* in front of *baccalaureate* may connote to some that the degrees awarded by colleges are not of the same stature as the baccalaureate degrees awarded by universities, it may be well to expunge this term from the formal lexicon of postsecondary credentials. The extent to which the actual learning experience follows a more experiential or inductive approach would then simply reflect an operational decision in program design at the program level. As noted, programs might vary along this dimension within both postsecondary sectors, but likely a significantly higher proportion of baccalaureate programs would have the applied orientation in the colleges than in the universities. This appears to be the case in the United States, where the term *applied* is not required to be affixed to baccalaureate programs in the colleges, and its absence does not seem to cause any problems.

In spite of the elusiveness of the underlying concept, the applied nature of baccalaureate degrees offered by community colleges is an important aspect of postsecondary education in Canada for two reasons. First, its presence may cause many individuals to be attracted to postsecondary education and to succeed in it, who would not otherwise be attracted or successful; and second, it might result in the production of graduates who bring practical, job-ready skills and knowledge to the workforce that make them highly valued and productive. It thus becomes important to consider how to organize baccalaureate education institutionally in a way that will facilitate or preserve this characteristic.

Concluding Comments: The Future of the Applied Baccalaureate Degree

Within the past two to three decades there has been great interest in many jurisdictions around the world in enabling community colleges, technical institutes, and similar types of postsecondary institutions to award applied baccalaureate degrees (Clark, Moran, Skolnik, & Trick, 2009; Taylor, Ferreira, Machado, & Santiago, 2008). The motivation for doing this has in large part been to provide a supply of workers for industry who possess a more advanced level of applied knowledge and skills that is thought to be essential to a modern economy. These applied baccalaureate programs build not only upon the expertise and curricular foundations of community colleges and technical institutes, but also on the ethos, traditions, and values of the institutions—which include their commitment to experiential and inductive learning. As a consequence, it is likely that applied baccalaureate programs provide an alternative route to baccalaureate attainment for some individuals who would not complete a baccalaureate degree if the traditional academic baccalaureate were the only route available.

There are some indications that the applied baccalaureate degrees awarded by community colleges and technical institutes do not enjoy the same status as the baccalaureate degrees that are awarded by universities. For example, no Canadian institution that is eligible to offer both applied baccalaureate programs and academic baccalaureate programs has proposed a new applied program, and such institutions are often seen converting applied baccalaureate programs into academic baccalaureate programs. Also, postgraduate and professional schools in Canadian universities, as well as some professional associations, have shown ambivalence, if not hostility toward recognizing an applied baccalaureate degree as being the equivalent of an academic baccalaureate degree[7] (Skolnik, 2005). Further, several of the community colleges that are among those offering the largest numbers of applied baccalaureate programs have lobbied governments to allow them to become universities, albeit in most cases a new type of university that would continue to offer some of the programs traditionally associated with the community college.

Thus far, five of the six former community colleges that have become universities within the past five years have continued to be members of the Association of Canadian Community Colleges. The new universities in British Columbia have both a college and a university mandate, the latter described as that of being "special focus, teaching-oriented universities."

However much these new universities are enjoined to, or profess to, maintain some of their community college programs and values, converting community colleges that offer large numbers of applied baccalaureate programs into universities seems a poor way to deal with concerns about possible status differences between applied and academic baccalaureate degrees. The history of higher education in Canada suggests that the new universities are likely to emulate the older universities in adopting the research university model (Clark, Moran, Skolnik, & Trick, 2009). It is important to note that the research university model, as it exists in Canada and many other countries, includes a shift of goals from development of skills to development of the mind as Paquet has described; and a shift in the predominant method of learning from inductive learning to what Schopenhauer called the artificial method of learning. It is noteworthy that earlier attempts in Nova Scotia, British Columbia, and Ontario to maintain technical universities that embodied orientations and values closer to those of community colleges than research universities were not successful.

Moreover, the practice of converting the community colleges that award large numbers of applied baccalaureate degrees, and are among those with the strongest academic reputations, into universities tends to diminish political support for the applied baccalaureate degree and reduce opportunities for learners who seek this type of educational experience, and for employers who value graduates of this type of baccalaureate program. For example, in Alberta the change in institutional status of the four colleges and institutes, in the two largest cities, that had the largest numbers of applied baccalaureate programs has removed the strongest bases of political support for the applied degree and left the future of that degree somewhat in limbo. The likely consequence is a decrease in opportunities for baccalaureate attainment in the smaller communities of the province, and fewer graduates of a type of program that was judged to be meeting the needs of students and employers.

In British Columbia, a commission on postsecondary education recommended that community colleges no longer be allowed to award baccalaureate degrees (Plant, 2007). Although the government did not accept this recommendation, the conversion of so many former colleges into universities might have reduced the capacity of the college sector to successfully fight similar recommendations in the future. In February 2012, a commission established by the Government of Ontario to find ways of reducing public sector spending recommended that no new college baccalaureate programs be allowed. The commission argued that this recommendation would result in cost savings by "minimizing further duplication of programs" (Commission on the Reform of Ontario's Public Services, 2012, p. 247). Apparently the commission did not realize that an existing requirement for college baccalaureate programs is that they do not duplicate any university program. Nor did the commission appreciate how college and university baccalaureate programs are differentiated with respect to goals and methods of learning—as described in this chapter—and that college and university baccalaureate programs serve largely different populations of students (Higher Education Strategy Associates, 2012). It is too soon to tell how the government will respond to this recommendation, but without the shared interest of the colleges that offer the largest numbers of baccalaureate programs, the other colleges would be in a weaker position to oppose the recommendation.

A decrease in the number of student places in applied baccalaureate programs in colleges that is matched by a corresponding increase in the number of places in academic baccalaureate programs in universities would leave the total number of places in baccalaureate programs unchanged. However, accompanying this apparent constancy in numbers would be a reduction in the diversity of opportunities for different types of baccalaureate programs that serve students with different learning needs and interests (Skolnik, 2011).

For those who appreciate the value of the applied baccalaureate degree both to learners and to industry, it is advisable not to get too excited about alleged or apparent differences in status between applied and academic baccalaureate degrees. As V. Lynn Meek and colleagues have noted, in most higher education systems, there is a prestige hierarchy among types of postsecondary institutions, with the research universities sitting at the apex (Meek, Goedegebuure, Kivinen, & Risto, 1996). The applied nature of college baccalaureate programs can be an advantage for colleges, so long as they don't carry this type of differentiation from academic baccalaureate programs to the extreme that Alberta has done. Moreover, a danger for colleges in trying to make their baccalaureate programs too much like university programs is that the unique applied nature of the programs will be lost in the process, and with it a major part of the raison d'etre for the colleges to be offering baccalaureate programs. Although colleges and institutes in Canada have lived—and flourished—with this kind of institutional prestige hierarchy for a long time, there are some signs that the discrepancy in prestige between sectors has been narrowing. Government of Canada Budgets have recognized that colleges and institutes play a role in the nation's innovation and economic development strategies that is distinct from but parallel to the role played by the universities (Flaherty, 2011). For example, the most recent budget includes funding for industrial research chairs in colleges and institutes. In any case, the important point to keep in mind is that the applied baccalaureate degree awarded by community colleges and technical institutes and the academic baccalaureate degree awarded by the universities both serve important, though different, societal needs. Accordingly, a nation's higher education system will be stronger if it makes adequate provision for both types of degrees to be successful.

Notes

1. This is the author's estimate derived from institutional websites in Manitoba, where colleges have only recently had the opportunity to submit applications to offer baccalaureate programs, and in Alberta; from the website of Postsecondary Education Quality Assessment Board in Ontario (www.peqab.ca); and from the database for all postsecondary education programs in British Columbia (www.educationplanner.ca). The figures exclude two programs in Ontario that are in the process of being phased out, and the programs of former colleges that have recently become universities.

2. The Association of Canadian Community Colleges (ACCC) estimated that as of January 2011, 41 postsecondary institutions "with a community college mandate" were offering 230 baccalaureate programs (Association of Canadian Community Colleges, 2011). Most of the difference between the author's and the ACCC estimates is due to the latter's inclusion of the programs of the former community colleges that have become universities.

3. A community college in Ontario has proposed a bachelor of interdisciplinary studies program that would enable students who have done a two-year career program in a community college to complete a bachelor's degree in two more years of general and career-related studies. This program would be similar to the university transfer model of the applied baccalaureate degree described by Townsend, Bragg, and Ruud (2008). No universities in Canada currently offer such a baccalaureate degree completion option for graduates of two-year career programs in community colleges. A description of the proposed program can be found on the website of the

Postsecondary Education Quality Assessment Board (www.peqab.ca/Publications/Consents/SenecaInterdisWeb.pdf).

4. The author thanks Mike Sherlock for acquainting him with Schopenhauer's essay on education.

5. The author is indebted to David Trick for this observation. Charles Pascal points out that both individual differences among students in regard to learning styles and the nature of the subject matter to be learned should be major considerations in determining the appropriate mix of different pedagogical approaches in colleges and in universities. He further suggests that opportunities for inductive learning should be prominent in most if not all learning settings (Pascal, personal communication, May 9, 2011).

6. The author wishes to thank Richard Van Loon for this example.

7. This is not unique to Canada. Nursing organizations in Australia campaigned vigorously against institutes of technical and further education (TAFEs) being allowed to offer baccalaureate programs in nursing ("TAFE Nursing Degrees Spark Protest," 2008).

References

Achtenhagen, F., & Grubb, W. N. (1999). Vocational and occupational education: Pedagogical complexity, institutional diversity. In V. Richardson (Ed.), *Handbook of research on teaching* (4th ed., pp. 604–639). Washington, DC: American Educational Research Association.

Alberta Advanced Education and Technology. (2011). *Applied degrees—enrolment and graduate outcomes.* Edmonton, AB: Advanced Education and Technology.

Alberta Ministry of Advanced Education and Career Development. (2007). *Roles and mandates policy framework for Alberta's publicly funded advanced education system.* Edmonton, AB: Ministry of Advanced Education and Career Development.

Association of Canadian Community Colleges. (2011). *Transferability and postsecondary pathways: The role of Canadian colleges and institutes.* Ottawa: ACCC. Accessed from http://www.accc.ca/ftp/pubs/studies/201104TransferabilityReport.pdf

British Columbia Ministry of Advanced Education. (2008). *Degree program review criteria and guidelines.* Accessed from www.aved.gov.bc.ca/degree_authorization/documents.degree_program_criteria.pdf

British Columbia Ministry of Regional Economic and Skills Development. (2010). *Degree authorization.* Accessed from http://www.aved.gov.bc.ca/degree-authorization/

Campus Alberta Quality Council. (2010). *Handbook: Quality assessment and quality assurance.* Accessed from http://www.caqc.gov.ab.ca/pdfs/Handbook_April_2010(2).pdf

Carr, B. (2001). The university-college system in British Columbia, Canada. *CCBA Beacon, 2*(1), 2–7.

Clark, I. D., Moran, G., Skolnik, M. L., & Trick, D. (2009). *Academic transformation: The forces reshaping higher education in Ontario.* Kingston, ON: Queen's University School of Policy Studies & McGill-Queen's University Press.

Colleges Ontario. (2009). *A new vision for higher education in Ontario: Submitted by the presidents of Ontario's 24 public colleges.* Toronto, ON: Colleges Ontario.

Commission on the Reform of Ontario's Public Services. (2012). *Public services for Ontarians: A path to sustainability and excellence.* Toronto, ON: Queen's Printer for Ontario.

Dennison, J. D. (1997). Higher education in British Columbia, 1945–1995: Opportunity and diversity. In G. A. Jones (Ed.), *Higher education in Canada: Different systems, different perspectives* (pp. 31–58). New York, NY: Garland.

Donohue, M. M. (2010). *Transfer of learning from the classroom to the cooperative education workplace in a baccalaureate program in an Ontario college of applied arts and technology* (Unpublished doctoral dissertation). University of Toronto. Accessed from http://hdl.handle.net/1807/26169

Flaherty, J. M., Minister of Finance. (2011). *The next phase of Canada's Economic Action Plan: A low-tax plan for jobs and growth.* Ottawa, ON: Ministry of Finance. Accessed from http://www.budget.gc.ca/2011/plan/Budget2011-eng.pdf

Government of Alberta. (2011). *Study in Alberta.* Accessed from http://www.studyinalberta.ca/post-secondary/psprograms.aspx#applied

Grubb, W. N., & Associates. (1999). *Honoured but invisible. An inside look at teaching in community colleges.* New York, NY: Routledge.

Higher Education Strategy Associates. (2012). *Changing times, changing places: The global evolution of the bachelor's degree and the implications for Ontario.* Toronto, ON: Higher Education Quality Council of Ontario.

Kolb, D. A. (1984). *Experiential learning: Experience as the source of learning and development.* Englewood Cliffs, NJ: Prentice-Hall.

Meek, V. L., Goedegebuure, L., Kivinen, O., & Risto, R. (1996). Conclusion. In V. L. Meek, L. Goedegebuure, O. Kivinen, & R. Risto (Eds.), *The mockers and the mocked: Comparative perspectives on differentiation, convergence, and diversity in higher education* (pp. 206–236). Guildford, Surrey: Pergamon.

Paquet, G. (2006). *Savoirs, savoir-faire, savoir-être: In praise of professional wroughting and wrighting. A think-piece prepared for Campus 2020—an inquiry into the future of British Columbia's postsecondary education system.* Victoria, BC: Ministry of Advanced Education. Available at http://gouvernance.ca/publications/06-18.pdf.

Plant, G. (2007). *Campus 2020: Thinking ahead: The report. Access & excellence. The Campus 2020 plan for British Columbia's postsecondary system.* Victoria, BC: Ministry of Advanced Education.

Postsecondary Education Quality Assessment Board. (2010). *Handbook for Ontario colleges applying for ministerial consent under the Postsecondary Education Choice and Excellence Act, 2000.* Accessed from http://www.peqab.ca/Publications/HNDBKCAAT2010.pdf

Postsecondary Education Quality Assessment Board. (2011). *Completed applications*. Accessed from http://www.peqab.ca/completed.html

Provincial Access Committee. (1988). *Access to advanced education and job training in British Columbia*. Victoria, BC: Ministry of Advanced Education.

Rothblatt, S. (1993). The limits of Osiris: Liberal education in the English-speaking world. In S. Rothblatt & B. Wittrock (Eds.), *The European and American university since 1800: Historical and sociological essays* (pp. 19–73). Cambridge, UK: Cambridge University Press.

Russell, A. (2010). *Update on the community college baccalaureate: Evolving trends and issues*. Washington, DC: American Association of State Colleges and Universities. Accessed from http://www.congressweb.com/aascu/docfiles/AASCU_Update_Community_College_Baccalaureate.pdf

Schopenhauer, A. (2005). On education. In The Pennsylvania State University (Ed.), *The essays of Arthur Schopenhauer: Studies in pessimism, Volume 4* (translated by T. Bailey Saunders, 51–58). Accessed from http://www2.hn.psu.edu/faculty/jmanis/schopenhauer/Schopenhauer-4.pdf

Skolnik, M. L. (2005). The community college baccalaureate in Canada: Addressing accessibility and workforce needs. In D. L. Floyd, M. L. Skolnik, & K. P. Walker (Eds.), *The community college baccalaureate: Emerging trends and policy issues* (pp. 49–72). Sterling, VA: Stylus.

Skolnik, M. L. (2009). Theorizing about the emergence of the community college baccalaureate. *Community College Journal of Research and Practice, 33*(2), 125–150.

Skolnik, M. L. (2011). Re-conceptualizing the relationship between community colleges and universities using a framework drawn from the study of jurisdictional conflict between professions. *Community College Review, 39*(4), 352–375.

TAFE Nursing Degrees Spark Protest. (2008, September 5). *The Australian online*. Accessed from http://www.theaustralian.com.au/higher-education/tafe-nursing-degrees-spark-protest/story-e6frgcjx-1111117402604

Taylor, J. S., Brites Ferreira, J., de Lourdes Machado, M., & Santiago, R. (Eds.). (2008). *Non-university higher education in Europe*. Dordrecht, NL: Springer.

Townsend, B. K., Bragg, D. D., & Rudd, C. M. (2008). *The adult learner and the applied baccalaureate: National and state-by-state inventory*. Office of Community College Research and Leadership, University of Illinois at Urbana-Champaign. Accessed from http://occrl.ed.uiuc.edu/Projects/lumina/AppBaccInventory.pdf

Walker, K. P., & Floyd, D. L. (2005). Applied and workforce baccalaureates. In D. L. Floyd, M. L. Skolnik, & K. P. Walker (Eds.), *The community college baccalaureate: Emerging trends and policy issues* (pp. 95–102). Sterling, VA: Stylus.

10

A VIRTUAL PATHWAY TO BACCALAUREATE COMPLETION

Lisa Romano-Arnold and Marie Cini

In years past, community college students wishing to pursue a baccalaureate degree had no choice but to matriculate to a traditional, residential brick-and-mortar institution. Before the focus on access and convenience for nontraditional students, this transfer process created hardships for most adults seeking to finish their degree. Adult students had to juggle the time constraints of work and family to attend evening classes or access support offices that closed at the end of the regular workday. Moreover, students in rural areas or those in the military had no options for completing their degrees. The traditional brick-and-mortar model is not conducive for adult students with complex lives who wish to pursue a baccalaureate degree. This educational gap spawned a variety of nontraditional models of baccalaureate completion.

While face-to-face university offerings at or near community colleges are a positive move for students, online education is creating new educational opportunities for the 21st century learner. Students are no longer limited by time or place; community college students no longer have to leave their communities or even their homes to pursue a baccalaureate degree. They can enjoy the flexibility of pursuing their educational goals while balancing the demands of work and family. This chapter discusses both traditional transfer and online transfer processes and examines the problems, practices, and promise of virtual pathways to the baccalaureate.

The Transitioning Learner

Several types of 2 + 2 transfer pathways exist between community colleges and four-year institutions, with the objective of creating greater access to the baccalaureate degree for community college students. These transfer agreements may exist in the form of statewide agreements or simply between two institutions. They may include program articulations, guaranteed admission policies, campus transfer centers, and other similar best transfer practices.

However community college students shift from the community college to a baccalaureate institution, the move is still fraught with many potential barriers and risks that might be exaggerated within the context of the virtual learning path. Transfer practices often target the traditional, face-to-face learners, leaving nontraditional and online students without many of the tools necessary for successful transfer to the baccalaureate institution. In fact, the majority of college students today no longer fit the term *traditional* (National Center for Educational Statistics, as quoted in Center for American Progress & Council for Adult and Experiential Learners [hereafter CAP & CAEL], 2011). With college completion rates declining and an increased focus on creating seamless transfer pathways, colleges and universities need to ask: "How are we serving the nontraditional, online transfer student?"

Online 2 + 2 transfer agreements can be a crucial component in combating declining college completion rates at both the community college and baccalaureate institutions. Transfer agreements can create a seamless pathway for community college students matriculating to a four-year college or university. However, the days of "simple" 2 + 2 transfer agreements are obsolete because of the changing needs of today's student. Even with numerous efforts and resources dedicated to improving the transfer process, college completion rates among community college transfer students remains disappointing at both the associate and baccalaureate levels.

Approximately 65% of beginning community college students who transfer to a four-year institution transfer without an associate's degree (McCormick & Carroll, 1997). About 43% of those who transfer after earning an associate's degree obtain a bachelor's degree within five years, compared with 17% who transfer without an associate's degree (McCormick & Carroll, 1997). Community college students who transfer to the baccalaureate institution without earning an associate's degree prior to transfer are less likely to earn a bachelor's degree and may take a longer time to baccalaureate completion as compared with their associate degree–earning peers (Best & Gehring, 1993; McCormick & Carroll, 1997). The associate's degree–earning students also persisted at higher rates at the baccalaureate institution than their non-degree counterparts, 98% versus 88%, respectively (McCormick & Carroll, 1997). Associate's degree attainment appears to be a critical building block for future academic success, yet the majority of community college transfer students are transferring without having earned their associate's degree.

Outdated or insufficient transfer practices and policies that do not reflect the needs of today's nontraditional student may also contribute to low rates of baccalaureate completion, which still lag behind those of native four-year students (McCormick & Carroll, 1997). Native four-year students complete baccalaureate degrees at rates 15–20% higher than associate's degree–earning transfer students (Best & Gehring, 1993; Hills, 1965; McCormick & Carroll, 1997). This suggests that additional barriers exist for community college transfer students, even for those who transfer with the associate's degree.

Transfer Barriers for the Nontraditional Learner

The lack of transferability of credits is the number one reported barrier among transfer students (Glass & Bunn, 1998; King, 1993). This transfer barrier often delays bachelor's degree attainment or discourages students who then leave the educational environment altogether (Cardenas & Warren, 1991; Dougherty, 1987; King, 1993). Transfer policies and practices among postsecondary institutions in the United States are complicated, laborious, and no longer meet the needs of students or institutions (Cardenas & Warren, 1991; The College Board, 2008, p. 18). Many baccalaureate institutions are reluctant to accept transfer students, which is made apparent through unfriendly transfer credit policies (Dougherty, 1992). Some students may be required to retake an English or math course upon transferring because the baccalaureate institution might not accept such courses in transfer from a community college. It is problematic to forging successful 2 + 2 partnerships when one institution requires "most or all learning relevant to a degree to take place at their institution" (CAP & CAEL, 2011, p. 3).

The absence of an electronic transfer credit mechanism and electronic institutional credit evaluation database makes reviewing student transcripts arduous and labor intensive. Antiquated, manual institutional processing of transfer credit does not support a seamless transfer of credit, nor does it assist in the effective evaluation of transfer credits in a timely manner (The College Board, 2008). Students often do not receive an evaluation of their transfer credits until they pay the admission fee and enroll in courses at the transfer institution. Students risk duplicating course work, resulting in wasted time and money.

Geographical barriers to the baccalaureate degree continue to be problematic for community college students as well (King, 1993). In some rural
communities, access to higher education opportunities is almost nonexistent.
Face-to-face options are limited, leaving online learning as the only viable
option. Without preparation and assimilation into the online learning environment, students may struggle to be successful and are at risk of dropping
out. Other students may have local institutional access, but the major they
wish to pursue is not offered locally. Again, online learning becomes the
only option.

Limited finances and the lack of financial aid available to transfer students is another reported barrier to baccalaureate completion (Doughtery,
1992; King, 1993; The National Center for Public Policy and Higher Education [hereafter NCPPHE], 2011). Transfer students often experience sticker
shock upon matriculation from the community college to the four-year institution, because they are not prepared for the drastic increase in tuition rates.
Students are not generally well informed of the financial aid deadlines at the
baccalaureate institution or the proper paperwork to be completed to apply
for institutional scholarships and grants. Discouraged at the impending debt
they could be assuming through student loans, transfer students might limit
their enrollment because of their inability to afford the expense of earning a
bachelor's degree.

As described earlier in this chapter, a major yet often misunderstood
barrier to baccalaureate completion is that many community college students
most often fail to complete an associate's degree prior to transferring to a
four-year institution. Some transfer agreements promote transfer after earning only 45 credits at the community college. Most associate's degrees consist
of at least 60 credits. Research (Best & Gehring, 1993; McCormick & Carroll, 1997) indicates that this early transfer behavior may be detrimental to
the goal of earning a bachelor's degree, with non-associate's-degree earners
being more at risk for departure from college. Transfer agreements should
be built around associate's degree completion, a crucial building block for
baccalaureate completion.

Although institutions have increased the promotion of 2 + 2 transfer
opportunities, many admission policies are still ambiguous and opaque,
causing confusion and frustration for students (The College Board, 2008).
For instance, some 2 + 2 transfer agreements promote guaranteed admission
to a state university or university system for students transferring from any
one of the state's community colleges. Usually students must transfer with a
certain number of credits earned and a specific GPA. What is misleading is

that admittance may only be guaranteed to the institution but not to a particular college or program within the institution, such as an accounting program. Community college students need clear information from advising staff and Web- and print-based materials prior to transferring in order to make a well-informed decision about the next step in their education. Transfer policies are unfamiliar territory for many community college students; therefore, strong support systems are needed to ensure a smooth transition (King, 1993).

Importantly, students transferring from a traditional face-to-face instructional format may experience additional transitional difficulties if they transfer into an online learning environment at the baccalaureate institution. Although online education has its benefits, it alone is not a panacea to fulfill the needs of today's learners. Convenience and flexibility, the primary cornerstones of online education, do not ensure success without appropriate student support services. Students who choose to be online learners face a multitude of challenges, including low levels of skill with technology, the potential isolation that might ensue from the lack of physical classroom interaction with fellow students and faculty, and the lack of motivation to "attend class." Transfer students might experience assimilation and adjustment issues to this different learning format, which could amplify the effects of transfer shock.

Transfer Shock

The institutional barriers discussed previously might be contributing factors to transfer shock, which itself might be a significant barrier in 2 + 2 transfer models. *Transfer shock* is a term coined by John Hills (1965) to describe the occurrence of a decline in GPA during the first two semesters at the baccalaureate institution compared with the final GPA at the community college. In addition to a dip in GPA, the concept of transfer shock has been expanded to include increased time to degree, decline in graduation rates, and increase in dropout rates (Knoell & Medsker, 1965; Rhine, Milligan, & Nelson, 2000; Stirewalt, as cited in Glass & Bunn, 1998).

Although data indicate that most students' GPAs bounce back after the first two semesters after transferring, this dip in GPA is not apparent in their four-year native counterparts (Hills, 1965). Theories as to why transfer shock occurs generally focus on the transition and adjustment a student makes from the community college to the university. Transfer shock is theorized to be the result of a combination of academic and societal variables that affect the transfer experience (Stirewalt, as cited in Glass & Bunn, 1998). Both student behaviors and institutional policy can impact a transfer student's ability to persist in transitioning from the community college to the baccalaureate institution, ultimately affecting the probability of completion.

Alexander Astin (1970) and Vincent Tinto (1975) have made significant contributions to the study of college student engagement and departure. Although most of their work is based on the traditional, native, four-year students, their concepts can be useful when studying community college transfer students as well. The overarching theme of their work is that students who persist are more engaged within the college environment. Those who fail to assimilate into their new collegiate environment tend to drop out. Characteristics of students most likely to drop out include those who (a) live off campus, (b) work off campus and are often employed full time, (c) those who experience limited engagement with faculty outside of the classroom as well as limited engagement in campus activities. This is often the description of typical, nontraditional community college online learners.

Another aspect of assimilation difficulty upon transfer can be attributed to the sophomore slump. Laurie Schreiner and Jerry Pattengale (2000) identify that sophomore students may become disengaged from the college community, resulting in a college experience that is contradictory to the development of engaged learners. They become less active in the classroom and within academic campus activities and retreat more into social activities to establish a sense of belonging. Second-year students are most in need of support services and opportunities for college involvement that support the development of academic and social adjustment to promote successful transfer to and involvement at the baccalaureate institution. There is a lack of college programming geared toward sophomore students to prepare them for the next milestone within their education, such as transferring into a baccalaureate program.

In sum, community college transfer students are more at risk for departure from college than their native four-year counterparts. Community college transfer students not only encounter structural barriers in transfer, which their four-year counterparts do not, but transfer students also experience the challenges of assimilation and adjustment both as community college freshmen and again as juniors at the baccalaureate institution (Romano-Arnold, 2012). Although many colleges and universities concentrate on the first-year student experience, more programming needs to address the challenges faced by community college sophomores. Community colleges and baccalaureate institutions should work together to provide transfer programming that fosters positive assimilation opportunities for successful transfer and matriculation into the baccalaureate environment. With the rise of online programs, future research studying the impact of online learning in relation to transfer shock would also be beneficial.

Promising Practices in Online 2 + 2 Partnerships

Today's 2 + 2 transfer agreement calls for a holistic approach to serving the needs of a diverse transfer student population within a diverse learning environment of various course delivery methods. Institutions would do well to develop a comprehensive transfer strategy, composed of interlocking programs and services to promote successful transfer and assimilation not only into the baccalaureate environment but also into the online environment. Successful partnerships remove barriers and provide opportunities for 2 + 2 completion, helping to achieve the Completion Challenge (American Association of Community Colleges [hereafter AACC], 2011). However, without also providing a package of support services relevant to online learners, universities allow students to flounder as they seek methods to become successful. The following provides five examples of institutions/systems that have established promising practices for 2 + 2 transfer agreements that can help remove transfer barriers for the online learner.

University of Maryland University College (UMUC), a 2 + 2 partner with more than 80 community colleges across the country, including all 16 Maryland community colleges, has developed the Alliance. The Alliance is a national, comprehensive 2 + 2 transfer program focused on successful student transfer and degree completion. At the heart of the Alliance lies program-to-program articulations, transfer-friendly credit policies, featuring an automated transcript evaluation process, scholarships for transfer students, and personalized transfer advising available live on the community college campus or virtually via computer videoconferencing or e-mail. With a focus on the Completion Challenge, a new reverse transfer initiative has been implemented that encourages the student to transfer UMUC credits back to their home community college to establish associate's degree completion. Last, specific programs and services are directed toward community college students up to a year prior to transferring, to encourage successful assimilation and adjustment upon matriculation at UMUC. Many of these programs are geared toward the online learner.

Transfer students interested in UMUC's online programs have the ability to participate in virtual events, including an open house, new-student orientation, and an academic "meet and greet" event. Each virtual event provides students with the ability to experience a virtual setting to recognize if online learning is a suitable vehicle for their learning style. In addition, prospective students can sign up for a free, weeklong "test-drive" of an online course before enrolling as a student. UMUC 411 was developed to help prospective online students experience an online course and assimilate into the online environment in a pressure-free setting. This program was created to manage expectations of what the online learning environment truly is, especially for traditional face-to-face learners and those unsure of their abilities to successfully learn within a virtual environment. Students have the opportunity to interact with fellow prospective students, academic advisors, faculty members, alumni, and other members of the UMUC community, as well as navigate through a real online classroom environment.

In addition to online learning preparation, UMUC provides student support services virtually to students around the globe. Students can take advantage of online tutoring, an effective writing center, advising offered through Skype, instant chats and e-mail, job fairs, mentoring, student clubs, and more. Institutions evolving their offerings to include online learning must also include online student support services to serve the student their full academic lifecycle. Virtual student services offer the same conveniences as online learning; for example, students may be more inclined to seek beneficial assistance such as academic advising if they do not have to wait in line or take off from work.

Rio Salado College (RSC) is the largest public, two-year provider of online education in the United States. In partnership with several colleges and universities, RSC has embarked on an innovative 2 + 2 transfer option called Communiversity. As a higher education center serving rural communities in Arizona, Communiversity provides a seamless transfer pathway to the baccalaureate degree as well as a doorway to online education. Students can begin taking face-to-face classes and then transition to hybrid classes before enrolling in fully online courses. Communiversity sites in Surprise, and Queen Creek, Arizona, provide students with the face-to-face student services that many students need during their initial enrollment at the community college and then again during the transfer process to the baccalaureate institution. At Communiversity, students enjoy flexible transfer policies that allow up to 90 credits in transfer along with program articulation agreements. Students can also earn a certificate, associate's, bachelor's, and master's degrees all through the Communiversity partnering institutions. As a part of the 2 + 2 agreement, four-year partners of Communiversity provide guaranteed admission agreements to students transferring from partnering community colleges.

Ozarks Technical Community College features OTC Online (OTCO), a virtual campus experiencing tremendous growth of 37% since fall 2009 (Ozarks Technical Community College, 2011). Through OTCO, students can transfer into specific online 2 + 2 transfer agreements with agreement benefits easily accessible on OTCO's website. Features of the agreements include articulated programs, waiver of application fees at the baccalaureate institutions, as well as special transfer scholarships and student tuition discounts. Twitter feeds provide up-to-date information of when transfer representatives are available to meet with OTCO students either virtually or face-to-face. For prospective OTCO students, a video demonstrating an online class is available to help them gain an understanding of how the online environment works. Students have the ability to access both live and online student services. This blended approach to student learning demystifies the online learning environment and creates access to the online platform in a student-safe, controlled environment.

These institutions described previously exemplify best practices in 2 + 2 transfer partnerships and demonstrate many key principles of successful transfer agreements as identified by Jan Ignash and Barbara Townsend (1991). First, at these institutions, the community college and the baccalaureate provider are equal partners in offering the first two years of a baccalaureate degree. Both institutions thus honor the transferability of course work, not just from two-year to four-year but also four-year to two-year in the case of reverse transfer. The authors next identify that baccalaureate institutions should treat transfer students as they do native students. Often the receiving institution treats transfer students as interlopers, which is reflected in practices such as requiring transfer students to retake course work previously taken at the community college or not providing them equal access to major courses. Transfer students should not be penalized for beginning their studies at a community college.

Another key to successful partnerships is to develop program-to-program articulations with faculty involvement (Ignash & Townsend, 1991). This principle removes the number one transfer barrier: the loss of credit upon transfer. It also engages faculty communication at both the community college and baccalaureate institution, further strengthening the partnership and providing better program alignment. Finally, successful partnerships monitor student outcomes to evaluate the effectiveness of the partnership.

Baccalaureate institutions need to do a better job of reporting the outcomes of transfer students at their institutions and share that data with the transferring community college. Tracking the performance of these students can provide valuable information on transfer patterns and practices of students, the effectiveness of institutional transfer policies and can also help institutions identify best practices in transfer.

The Western Interstate Commission for Higher Education (WICHE) developed a best practices in transfer and articulation report recently, focusing on core concepts to ensure successful 2 + 2 partnerships. WICHE highlighted collaboration, communication, and transparency in transfer. Although there has been much publicity on best practices in transfer, there is little published on the outcomes of these practices. As Ignash and Townsend (1991) recommend, the WICHE report also includes evaluation and assessment of transfer practices as an essential component to successful 2 + 2 partnerships.

The Maricopa Community Colleges (MCC), of which Rio Salado is a part, requires that participating 2 + 2 partners provide yearly reports on student outcomes pertaining to students who transferred from the MCC system. Baccalaureate institutions are also mandated to send transfer surveys to the respective students, so MCC can measure the success of their partnerships. More community colleges should have access to this type of data from their partnering four-year institutions. The MCC 2 + 2 partnership also calls for an internal yearly review of the baccalaureate partner institutions to ensure the institutions are engaged in MCC transfer events and activities, program articulations are updated, and to review the results of the partner assessments to evaluate the effectiveness of that particular 2 + 2 partnership. This model promotes accountability and supports partnership effectiveness to better improve transfer pathways for students.

Although online course delivery in particular has increased access to the baccalaureate degree, access alone is not enough to facilitate completion. Online education entails more than offering Web-based programs. It requires engaging the student through a comprehensive package of online student services to promote successful persistence and completion. To serve community college students, this means developing virtual transitional support programs and services to mitigate the effects of transfer shock.

Summary and Conclusions

Within the 21st century learning environment, two trends in higher education are evident: Online enrollments continue to increase as do enrollments at U.S. community colleges. More than 20% of students in the United States are enrolled in at least one online course (National Center for Education Statistics, 2011). Of the nearly 4 million online students in the country, 80% are pursuing undergraduate education (Allen & Seaman, 2008, p. 5). As online enrollments grow, so, too, does the number of students who choose to begin their postsecondary education at a community college. Community colleges enroll approximately 44% of the country's undergraduate student population with enrollments having increased by more than one million students from fall 2008 to fall 2010 (AACC, 2011). With online education enabling access to the baccalaureate degree, a tremendous opportunity exists to create synergies between online learning and transfer pathways to promote student success.

Throughout the country, many examples of 2 + 2 transfer best practices are being identified, such as transfer student orientation, campus transfer centers, and summer bridge programs. However, the effectiveness of these programs is largely unknown, owing to the lack of assessment and evaluation procedures in place. In order to combat the issue of declining college completion rates, a more comprehensive and strategic approach to creating 2 + 2 transfer agreements must be implemented. A key to the success of these new comprehensive agreements is the use of enabling technologies.

In addition, with online enrollments continuing to soar, postsecondary institutions must remedy the challenges facing online learners. Institutions must prepare students for the demands of online coursework along with managing their expectations regarding the effort they must put forth to be successful. This preparation includes introducing students to online learning at the community college prior to transferring to a baccalaureate institution. This could include the requirement of enrolling in at least one Web-enhanced, face-to-face course, a hybrid course, or a fully online class. In addition, students should be encouraged to take advantage of virtual student services at the community college, such as online registration, accessing grades through the student portal, and even obtaining transfer information through webinars or Skype advising appointments. A traditional face-to-face learner at the community college who transfers to an online baccalaureate institution may encounter adjustment and assimilation issues not only with learning how to adapt to the new policies and procedures at the baccalaureate institution, but also with adapting to a new online academic environment.

Transfer partnerships must be centered on completion at both the community college and at the baccalaureate institution. Programmatic articulations should include associate's degree requirements as a prerequisite so that students transfer with that important credential. For nontraditional students, that associate's degree could be their safety net in case "life happens," as it so often does for adult students. For transfer students in general, it means shortening time to baccalaureate completion. Associate's degree attainment is the most crucial indicator for baccalaureate success (Best & Gehring, 1993; McCormick & Carroll, 1997).

Assessment and evaluation must also be a part of the 2 + 2 process. Benchmarks should be created to measure the effectiveness of newly created transfer initiatives. For example, institutions could measure the existence of transfer shock at their institutions by comparing first- to second-semester GPA's of new community college transfer students and comparing it to the ending GPA at the community college. A dip in the first semester GPA will identify if there is a presence of transfer shock. Then comparing first-semester to second-semester GPA will identify if there is GPA recovery. If there is a presence of transfer shock, baccalaureate institutions will be aware that their transfer students may have some assimilation difficulties and can then begin to build additional programming with the community college to promote transfer-student success.

For the first time in our history, we may have a generation whose educational attainment does not surpass that of their parents, unless we take steps to change this reality. Baccalaureate institutions are likely to benefit from embracing community college transfer students. Likewise, community colleges can serve their students by embracing a diversity of learning formats and encouraging students to participate in the online learning environment. The future of education is about serving students; those who can provide an affordable, quality education while offering flexible learning options are in the best position to serve students.

References

Allen, I. E., & Seaman, J. (2008). *Staying the course: Online education in the United States, 2008.* Sloan-C and Sloan Consortium. Retrieved from http://sloanconsortium.org/

American Association of Community Colleges. Retrieved April 9, 2011, from http://www.aacc.nche.edu/

Astin, A. W. (1970). College influence: A comprehensive view. *Contemporary Psychology.* Retrieved from http://www.apa.org/journals/cnt.html

Best, G. A., & Gehring, D. D. (1993). The academic performance of community college transfer students at a major state university in Kentucky. *Community College Review, 21*(2), 32–41. doi:10.1177/009155219302100205

Cardenas, R., & Warren, E. (1991). Community college access: Barriers and bridges. *New Directions for Community Colleges, 74*, 15–22. doi:10.1002/cc.36819917405

Center for American Progress & Council for Adult and Experiential Learners. (2011, June). *Articulation agreements and prior learning assessments: Tools to help 21st century students achieve their postsecondary education goals and keep America competitive.* Washington, DC: Author.

The College Board Commission on Access, Admissions and Success in Higher Education. (2008). *Coming to our senses: Education and the American future.* Retrieved from http://collegeboard.com/

Dougherty, K. (1987). The effects of community colleges: Aid or hindrance to socioeconomic attainment? *Sociology of Education, 60*(2), 86–103. doi:10.2307/2112584

Dougherty, K. J. (1992). Community colleges and baccalaureate attainment. *Journal of Higher Education, 63*(2), 188–214. Retrieved from http://www.eric.ed.gov/

Glass, J., & Bunn, C. E. (1998). Length of time required to graduate for community college students transferring to senior institutions. *Community College Journal of Research and Practice, 22*(3), 239–261. Retrieved from http://www.eric.ed.gov/

Hills, J. R. (1965). Transfer shock—the academic performance of the junior college transfer. *Journal of Experimental Education, 22*(3), 202–215. Retrieved from http://www.eric.ed.gov/

Ignash, J. M., & Townsend, B. K. (1991). Statewide transfer and articulation policies: Current practices and emerging issues. In B. Townsend & S. Twombly (Eds.), *Community Colleges: Policy in the future context* (pp. 173–192). Westport, CT: Ablex.

King, M. C. (1993). Academic advising, retention, and transfer. *New Directions for Community Colleges, 82*, 21–31. doi:10.1002/cc.36819938204

Knoell, D. M., & Medsker, L. L. (1965). *From junior college to senior college: A national study of the transfer student.* Washington, DC: American Council on Education. Retrieved from http://www.eric.ed.gov/

McCormick, A., & Carroll, C. D. (1997). *Transfer behavior among beginning postsecondary students: 1989–94* (NCES 97-266). Washington, DC: National Center for Education Statistics, U.S. Department of Education. Retrieved from http://nces.ed.gov/

National Center for Education Statistics. (2011). Retrieved from http://nces.ed.gov

The National Center for Public Policy and Higher Education. (2011). *Affordability and transfer: Critical to increasing baccalaureate degree completion.* San Jose, CA.

Ozarks Technical Community College. (2011). Retrieved from http://www.otc.edu

Rhine, T. J., Milligan, D. M., & Nelson, L. R. (2000). Alleviating transfer shock: Creating an environment for more successful transfer students. *Community College Journal of Research and Practice, 24*(6), 443–453. Retrieved from http://www.eric.ed.gov/

Romano-Arnold, L. M. (2012). *Mitigating the effects of transfer shock among community college transfer students: Creating an advising model framework* (Unpublished doctoral dissertation). University of Maryland University College, Adelphi, Maryland.

Schreiner, L. A., & Pattengale, J. (2000). *Visible solutions for invisible students: Helping sophomores succeed. Monograph 31* (pp. 55–77). South Carolina University, Columbia National Resource Center for the Freshman Year Experience and Students in Transition.

Tinto, V. (1975). Dropout from higher education: A theoretical synthesis of recent research. *Review of Educational Research, 45*(1), 89–125. doi:10.2307/1170024

Western Interstate Commission for Higher Education. (2010). *Promising practices in statewide articulation and transfer systems* (Publication Number 2A373). Retrieved from www.wiche.edu/publications

11

THE UNIVERSITY
PARTNERSHIP AT LORAIN
COUNTY COMMUNITY
COLLEGE

Marcia J. Ballinger and John R. Crooks

S eventeen states have authorized community colleges to grant bachelor's degrees from their institutions, most often in applied areas (Gonzalez, 2011; Lewin, 2009). This has been and will continue to be used to address local workforce needs and increase educational attainment for the citizens of these states. Over a work life, individuals who have a bachelor's degree would earn on average $2.1 million—about one-third more than workers who did not finish college, and nearly twice as much as workers with only a high school diploma (Day & Newman, 2002). Thirty-three states do not allow community colleges to have the authority to grant the bachelor's degree to their students. Attempts within these states have been denied by either the legislature or their board of regents. How do institutions in large states such as Michigan and Ohio address the educational attainment issue without providing community college authorization to grant bachelor's degrees? They have created university centers on their campus. These centers provide area students with the opportunity to complete additional education on-site and often meet the needs of both the community and the residents. This is realized at the local level and is often initiated by the citizens of the community college district.

Lorain County Community College (LCCC), located in Elyria, Ohio, was an early innovator in the quest to bring baccalaureate degrees to its community in the mid-1990s. During the past 15 years, the University Partnership has provided an opportunity for people in Lorain County to earn a bachelor's or master's degree. It is an opportunity for the community to illustrate its belief in higher education, quality of life, and that the residents are truly concerned with the future viability of the region.

Comprehensive community colleges, such as LCCC, build mission and vision with internal and external stakeholders. LCCC works hard to deliver on its four cornerstones—educational attainment, economic development, building cultural engagement and opportunities, and connecting with the community. LCCC believes strongly that, to drive economic growth in the region, it must help in creating the new jobs as well as providing the educational opportunity. The following illustrates how a group of citizens took ownership of their situation and made an innovative idea a reality.

Establishing the LCCC University Partnership

On November 15, 1994, more than 300 community residents gathered for the first phase of the three-part University Center Partnership Plan Summit. They joined together to explore the possibility of developing a new level of education for Lorain County through The Lorain County University Center Partnership Plan.

As LCCC developed its "Vision 2000" Strategic Plan, it assessed the local community's educational needs. Many issues surfaced, including low educational attainment for Lorain County residents. In fact, the 1990 Census data confirmed that among Lorain County's adults 25 years of age or older, only 12% had completed four or more years of college. This was the lowest educational attainment within a seven-county northeast Ohio region, consisting of Cuyahoga, Geauga, Lake, Medina, Lorain, Portage, and Summit Counties. Lorain County fell 29% below Ohio's 17% average and 40% below the national average of 20%. Lorain County's 4.3% educational attainment rate for holders of graduate and professional degrees was well below Ohio's 5.9% average and also lagged behind the national 7.2% average.

The need for providing expanded access to upper-division and graduate course work for the place-bound Lorain County resident was never clearer. Consider these 1994 factors:

The economic future of Lorain County was becoming more dependent on high-skill jobs requiring increased educational levels.

When compared with northeast Ohio, Lorain County trailed the region's per capita income level by twelve cents on the dollar.

Compared with eight other benchmark regions like Grand Rapids, Minneapolis, Buffalo, Cincinnati, Indianapolis, Greenville, Dallas, and Cleveland, Lorain County had the lowest per capita income.

Compared with the same benchmark regions, Lorain County ranked in the upper half in percentage of associate's degree holders and last in the percentage of bachelor's and graduates with professional degrees.

Lorain County is the largest county in Ohio without a public university or a university branch.

More than half of all new jobs created by the year 2000 would require postsecondary education or training.

One in four new jobs will require a four-year degree.

Almost half of the existing jobs in all categories of the nation's workforce will be significantly altered over the next 20 years to require additional formalized education and training.

Of the projected workforce for the year 2000, 80% were already beyond high school age and in the workforce.

During the initial development of the University Center Partnership Plan concept, LCCC's Joint Center for Policy Research conducted a comprehensive research effort in the summer of 1993 and fall of 1994. Fifteen focus groups were conducted with 150 participants. Specific target populations reached through this were LCCC students from transfer programs as well as direct entry programs, alumni, faculty, high school students, and homeowners in the county. Interviews were conducted in the workplace with 385 workers who represented an industry and occupational mix of Lorain County's workforce. Of those interviewed, 90% responded favorably to the concept of the University Center Partnership Plan in Lorain County.

Twenty-five in-depth interviews with county employers, labor leaders, economic development leaders, and other visionaries in the county were also conducted. Among their concerns was that greater diversity in the economic base was needed to draw and retain educated youth in the county. They also believed that an increase in the number of high-paying professional jobs was needed to improve wealth and enhance the quality of life. They believed the University Center plan would help achieve this. The plan was also taken to more than 150 community groups, including churches, civic organizations, labor groups, and others. The presentation provided the participants with the opportunity to learn about the concept and then react to it. More than

2,000 surveys were returned and analyzed, and 98% of the respondents believed more Lorain County residents would earn four-year degrees if the University Center Partnership Plan became reality.

Economic Advantages

Attracting new business and creating more jobs exemplified the impact that the University Center Partnership Plan could have in our community. Lorain County's need to expand and diversify its economic base would be enhanced through the University Center plan. Summit participants indicated that an educated workforce is needed for Lorain County to attract the type of "growth" industries, "high-tech" jobs, and "better" service industries that the county was seeking. The plan was deemed to have the potential to be the solution to create a more educated and skilled workforce, which would allow workers to keep pace with degree requirements of today's job market. It would also provide additional opportunities for the workers to change careers. The University Center would not only enhance recruitment efforts for business, it was also viewed as an initiative that would help Lorain County retain current business and industry.

The summit participants also believed the University Center plan had the potential to stimulate small business development and enhance entrepreneurialism. It also held tremendous hope for the county's employers, by supplying a skilled workforce prepared for today's complex, global business environment.

In September 1994, Lorain County's business community established "bringing the University Center initiative to fruition" as its second priority in developing the county's strategies that reduce gaps or barriers to economic development. This planning effort, which was spearheaded by the Economic Development Committee of the Lorain County Chamber of Commerce, included participation by the chief executive officers and presidents of more than 50 companies. As they compared Lorain County against 10 benchmark regions that were selected across the United States, the following gaps were identified:

Lorain County ranked 6th among these regions across the nation in growth of business establishments.
Lorain County ranked 8th among benchmark regions across the nation in total employment growth.

The impact has been a steady growth in the personal per capita income for Lorain County residents. In 1995, the per capita income for Lorain County was $21,283, and in 2008 the per capita income was $33,123. This is a 55% increase over a 13 year period.

Benefits to the Community

From minimizing out-migration of Lorain County's educated individuals to improving the overall quality of life, the University Center Partnership Plan was deemed to have the potential to create significant benefits for the community. The plan enhanced the ability to keep both educated professionals and young people in the community. This would impact the future reservoir of knowledge for Lorain County. And the monetary advantages for Lorain County would be significant, because the tax base could expand through reduction of out-migration as well as higher earning potential and the enhanced economic base.

The intrinsic value placed on higher education locally would ultimately be improved with the University Center Partnership Plan in Lorain County. Additionally it could improve the overall quality of life through enhanced lifestyles, social life, and social structures. It would also instill a sense of pride in the community and make Lorain County a more marketable place to live and work. This plan symbolized Lorain County taking care of its own by creating an opportunity for upper-division educational programs in the community (see table 11.1).

TABLE 11.1
Lorain County Educational Attainment

Level of Attainment	1990	2000	2008
Associate's degree	11,066	12,828	17,315
Bachelor's degree	13,642	20,203	25,424
Graduate or professional degree	7,261	10,538	14,773
Percentages			
High school graduate or higher	75.28%	73.77%	87.90%
Bachelor's degree or higher	12.33%	16.57%	19.90%

Benefits to the Individual

When the Lorain County Community College University Partnership (UP) was designed, increasing educational attainment levels among Lorain County's residents was the overarching benefit emphasized for individuals. The place-bound adult student would no longer be penalized for his or her occupational and family constraints. The plan would bring the university experience to this community. In addition to the adult population, younger students might also receive more parental support to attend college or earn a four-year degree, and the students might find bachelor's degrees more attainable.

Increasing individual earning potential and improving the per capita income were also identified as potential benefits. The spring 1990 Census Bureau Statistics on educational attainment showed that the average monthly income for a bachelor's degree holder was $2,489 whereas the associate's degree holder earned an average of $1,879 per month. Over the lifetime of work, the difference between the average worker with a bachelor's degree and the worker with an associate's degree was nearly $300,000, and the difference between the average worker with a bachelor's degree and a worker with high school diploma was $500,000.

The University Center Partnership Plan would make advanced degrees more affordable to individuals. By spending the first two years at LCCC, individuals would significantly reduce their tuition for the advanced degree. Additionally, the savings that result from the elimination of room and board and travel expenses make the plan an attractive option. Convenient access enables students to continue working while going to college. Stimulating personal growth, individual self-esteem, personal pride, and self-reliance were also highlighted as benefits.

Set against that backdrop of community support and desire for bachelor's degree and master's degree options in Lorain County, the college went to voters in November 1995 to establish financial support for the University Partnership. Lorain County voters approved a 1.2 mill levy to establish the University Partnership by a 54% to 46% margin. A 1.5 mill replacement levy for continuing support of the University Partnership was approved by voters in November 2004, again by a 54% to 46% margin.

The University Partnership began in 1996 with 7 bachelor's degrees and 1 master's program, offered by 5 universities. That list has grown to 9 universities providing 30 bachelor's programs and 8 master's programs through the University Partnership program. Additional programs are being negotiated at this time, and it is expected that these numbers will continue to grow. An example of cost savings realized by students and their families is shown in table 11.2.

The 3 + 1 model is very attractive to students and can also be attractive to the four-year partner as well. This model is aimed at pooling resources between institutions to focus student recruitment and marketing on affordable 3 + 1 options. This would allow cobranding of higher education opportunities and afford all the benefits associated with this type of collegial behavior. It could allow the institutions to:

Build long-term loyalty among a larger constituent base.
Enhance the resource base.

TABLE 11.2
Cost for Attendance of a Variety of UP Programs at LCCC Versus University Partner as a Residential Student

College/University	Tuition and Room & Board for 4 years	Program Costs Through UP	Savings
Ashland University, BS in Education	$148,024	$36,979	$111,045
Bowling Green State University, BS in Biology	$70,952	$20,151	$50,801
Cleveland State University, BA in Psychology	$81,256	$21,466	$59,790
Kent State University, Bachelor of Business Administration	$72,704	$22,063	$50,641
Ohio University, Bachelor of Technical and Applied Studies	$82,296	$15,382	$66,914
University of Akron, BS in Sport Studies	$72,439	$20,749	$51,690
University of Toledo, BS in Computer Science & Engineering	$72,174	$30,138	$42,036
Youngstown State University, BS in Applied Science, Major in Allied Health	$61,405	$17,298	$44,107

Attract more students for all institutions.

Increase Northern Ohio's educational attainment level.

Send a positive message to partners and stakeholders.

Attract and retain the state's best and brightest to prevent brain drain.

The 3 + 1 arrangement is possible because of a focus on the alignment of learning outcomes between courses. The focus on the final year is on courses within the major and meeting any residence requirements the institution might require. This allows the greatest cost savings to students, maintains academic rigor, because course outcomes are matched and met, and builds a new set of alumni for both partnering institutions.

The current programs are:

UP BACHELOR PROGRAMS

3 + 1 Programs

Allied Health—(30 hours from YSU)

AMET—(32 hours from Akron)

Biology—(30 hours from BGSU)

Business—(33 hours from Kent)

CIS—(34 hours from Akron)

Criminal Justice—(30 hours from YSU)

Exercise Science—(32 hours from Akron)

Nursing—(32 hours from Akron)

Postsecondary Technical Education—(32 hours from Akron)

Psychology—(36 hours from CSU)

Sport Studies—(32 hours from Akron)

Technical and Applied Studies—(49 quarter hours from OU)

2.5 + 1.5 Programs

Public Safety Management (47–48 credit hours from CSU, 81–82 from LCCC)—**63% LCCC**

Urban Services Administration (48 credit hours from CSU, 80 from LCCC)—**62% LCCC**

Urban Studies (47–48 credit hours from CSU, 79–80 from LCCC)—**62% LCCC**

Ashland University

Bachelor of Science in Education—Early Childhood Intervention Specialist (Pre-K–3)

Bachelor of Science in Education—Early Childhood Licensure (Pre-K–3)

Bachelor of Science in Education—Middle Childhood Licensure (4–9)

Bachelor of Science in Education-K–12 Intervention Specialist Mild/Moderate
Bachelor Plus for Teacher Licensure
Master of Science in Education major in Curriculum and Instruction
Master of Science in Education major in Educational Administration

Bowling Green State University

Bachelor of Science in Biology
Bachelor of Science in Environmental Science

Bowling Green State University–Firelands College Programs

Associate of Applied Science—Respiratory Care
Bachelor of Applied Health Science—Respiratory Care Specialist

Cleveland State University

Bachelor of Arts in Psychology
Bachelor of Arts in Public Safety Management
Bachelor of Arts in Nonprofit Administration (previously Urban Services
    Administration)
Bachelor of Arts in Urban Studies
Bachelor of Science in Electronics Engineering Technology
Bachelor of Science in Mechanical Engineering Technology
Master of Education with a specialization in Educational Technology
Certificate in Adult Learning and Development
Computer and Technology Teaching Endorsement

Hiram College

Bachelor of Arts in Accounting and Financial Management

Kent State University

Bachelor of Business Administration in Business Management with optional
    International Business Minor
Master of Business Administration
Master of Library and Information Science

Ohio University

Bachelor of Technical and Applied Studies

The University of Akron

Bachelor of Science in Automated Manufacturing Engineering Technology
Bachelor of Science in Computer Information Systems
Bachelor of Science in Emergency Management
Bachelor of Science in Exercise Science

Bachelor of Science in Nursing
Bachelor of Science in Postsecondary Technical Education
Bachelor of Science in Sports Studies
Bachelor of Science in Surveying and Mapping Technology
Master of Science in Nursing
Master of Science in Nursing (RN to MSN)

The University of Toledo

Bachelor of Science in Computer Science and Engineering
Bachelor of Science in Computer Science and Engineering Technology

Youngstown State University

Bachelor of Science in Applied Science—Allied Health
Bachelor of Science in Applied Science   Criminal Justice
Bachelor of Science in Applied Science—Public Health
Bachelor of Social Work
Master of Health and Human Services
Certificate in Health Care Management

In the first year of the University Partnership program, 257 students enrolled in programs offered by the partner colleges and universities. Two years later, that number jumped to 735 students. As of May 2011, 3,748 students have earned bachelor's or master's degrees through the University Partnership.

LCCC was able to expand its initial offerings from the 8 programs to the current 38 in the University Partnership, because it committed to the creation of a facility specifically for University Partnership courses to be held on campus. In October 1999, LCCC opened the 80,000-square-foot, three-story University Center building. The University Center gave LCCC a greater capacity to offer bachelor's and master's programs on its campus, because state-of-the-art technology was included that allows classes to be taught via two-way interactive video, the Internet, and in person.

Business Continues Its Support for the University Partnership

To support scholarship and incentive awards, install distance-learning technology in the University Center, and to generally secure the success of the University Partnership program, the LCCC Foundation launched a major gifts campaign in 1999. That campaign exceeded its original $5 million goal by raising nearly $8 million from area foundations, corporations, and individuals. Nearly $3.5 million of this support is represented through contributions ($50,000 or more) from members of the LCCC League of Partners, a growing group of corporations, which demonstrate significant leadership support through their contributions to the campaign.

The members of the League of Partners include companies like Ford Motor Company; Lorain National Bank; FirstMerit Bank, N.A.; Consumers Builders Supply; The Beckett Companies; P.C. Campana, Inc.; NACS, Inc.; Ridge Tool Company; and Invacare Corporation.

University Partnership Student Highlights and Comments

LCCC UP students have been named Toledo's top students twice since the University of Toledo joined the University Partnership program. Kaleb Brasee of Wakeman in 2004, and Mark McDermott of North Olmsted in 2009, were each named the top student in the University of Toledo's computer science and engineering bachelor's degree program. Both were chosen from among all of Toledo's students in the program, including those on Toledo's main campus.

Zenaida Ortiz, 23, from Lorain, earned an associate of early childhood education in May 2011 from LCCC and is currently enrolled in the early childhood education bachelor's degree program through Ashland University. When asked, "Why choose UP?" she responded:

> It is such an advantage to continue my education in the same place I completed my first goal. I believe that you don't have to go long distances to be able to get the same great education that the University Partnerships offers here at Lorain County Community College. I have been able to interact and learn from other students and teachers that are at the main campus while staying close to my home in Lorain. . . .
>
> Before I started my experience with Ashland University to obtain my bachelor's degree I had really set goals of what I was expecting and what my plan was after graduation. However, the faculty and the rich early childhood program has not changed but extended my initial goals. I always thought that my career would be to work with preschoolers, but now I feel that I am able to become not only a great preschool teacher, but teach any grade I want! I began to be excited about all the possibilities I have with my career option, and feel so empowered about how I will pursue my profession. The amazing thing is that I have only begun my *first* semester. I can't imagine what the rest will bring.

Chris Novick, 27, of Strongsville, earned an associate of science degree from LCCC and a bachelor of science in computer science and engineering from the University of Toledo through the UP in 2009. Chris is an engineer at Zin Technologies, which is a NASA contractor. He works on projects related to long-term spaceflight, primarily the International Space Station. Why choose UP?

> LCCC is significantly cheaper than a four-year university, and the education is high quality—some of my best professors were LCCC professors. If I had to do it all over again, I would still enroll in LCCC's UP program. The distance-learning classes, like quantum computing were handled very well. The LCCC staff was always on the ball making sure everything was in order—from making sure the equipment was up and running by the time I got to class every time, to making sure my tests got to me and back to UT on time. . . .
>
> I would be in significantly more debt, for one, as I would have had to [move] to a four-year university instead of being able to commute and work. I can't help but think having smaller class sizes helped make some of the more trying classes (like automata and data communications) easier to deal with.

Krystal Kinley, 23, of Grafton, is currently working on a bachelor's degree in social work from Youngstown State University through the UP. "The program offers real-world experience and the opportunity to build a network of contacts in the social services field," Kinley said.

Linda Gebhardt, of Avon Lake, moved up the teaching ranks, going from teaching preschool to elementary school, after graduating from Ashland University's bachelor's of science in education program through the UP in 2004. She now teaches at Redwood Elementary School in Avon Lake. Gebhardt said she chose LCCC's University Partnership because of "location, price and on-site daycare for my then-four-year-old son." She said she probably would not have returned to school if it weren't for the University Partnership. "The University Partnership was extremely important for me. Being a nontraditional student, I had family responsibilities to consider," Gebhardt said.

Paul McMasters, of Wellington, knows that today's global economy demands an unprecedented level of education to just keep up. That's why, more than 10 years ago, he advocated for the creation of Lorain County Community College's University Partnership program. Today he is a graduate of the Kent State University business administration bachelor's program located on the Lorain County Community College campus as a result of the partnership between the two institutions. This partnership created a 3 + 1 program that provided McMasters with the opportunity to enroll in LCCC classes for three years, to pay LCCC tuition, to enroll one year at Kent State University, and to graduate with a bachelor's degree without ever having to leave the LCCC campus in Elyria.

Like many working adults, McMasters was looking for a mechanism that would serve his needs of going to school while still meeting his family, career, and civic responsibilities in his local community. After receiving his baccalaureate, McMasters, employed as a program analyst for Analex at NASA Glenn Research Center, noted, "I received a position upgrade and pay raise in my current position" (Ballinger, 2006).

Lakeland Community College Establishes a University Center

Lakeland Community College, on the east side of Cleveland, Ohio, has built a University Center based on the LCCC model. The center opened in the fall of 2011 and is off to a fast start. Lakeland has created partnerships with the following institutions: Cleveland State University, Franklin University, Kent State University, Lake Erie College, Ohio University, The University of Akron, The University of Toledo, Ursuline College, and Youngstown State. About one-third of the programs that have been selected are the same as those offered at Lorain County Community College, allowing both the east and west sides of Cleveland greater access to higher education.

LCCC University Partnership Expands

LCCC has been very successful in developing several outreach centers throughout its service area and has received authorization from the Higher Learning Commission of the North Central Association for this activity. LCCC has now used this outreach center strategy to enhance and expand the University Partnership. The new center, located on a 6.8-acre site, in the county's eastern suburb of North Ridgeville, is poised to open in early 2013. This 40,000 + -square-foot, three-story Ridge Campus University Center will serve an expanded population of Lorain County adults who work in the adjacent Cuyahoga County. The center will focus on IT programs, such as computer information systems and services, CISCO, digital forensics, and health care simulation. In addition to these niche programs offered collaboratively among LCCC and its university partners, the center will also serve entrepreneurs through an extension of the college's business incubator. This new University Center Ridge Campus is positioned to address the following five priorities as delineated in LCCC's Vision 2015:

> Raise the community's participation and attainment in higher education.
> Prepare globally competent talent to compete in the innovation economy.
> Accelerate business and job growth to enhance regional competitiveness.
> Connect Lorain County with regional priorities and partners.
> Serve as a catalyst for enhanced community life.

Ohio State Senator Gayle Manning, a former North Ridgeville teacher, reinforced the importance of a community college expanding its university partnership offerings. As quoted in *The Sun News*, "Ohio's community colleges play an integral role in preparing students to compete in today's global economy, offering quality programs at an affordable price," State Senator Gayle Manning, R-13, said. "Building a new outreach center will allow LCCC to better serve students in the area" (Meaney, 2011).

Institutions of higher education (two-year and four-year) will play a significant role in ensuring Ohio's future economic success. They will serve their service district as an economic driver of the community as well as providing the region's social and cultural inspiration. This specific outreach center has a focus that aligns with Ohio's goal of transforming itself into a powerhouse of the "knowledge-based" economy that will define the 21st century. The North Ridgeville location is ideal and has the support of local, regional, and state leaders. The University Center Ridge Campus of Lorain County Community College combines the strengths of the community college (and its entrepreneurial spirit) and those of the four-year university (with mandatory co-op experiences) into a winning paradigm. It is the next step in the evolution of today's UP program.

Impact of LCCC University Partnership

The University Partnership has made a difference within the LCCC service district. LCCC's Joint Center for Policy Research surveys UP graduates every two years. The most recent graduate survey (2010) documents compelling numbers to support this endeavor:

> Eighty-six percent of the UP graduates enrolled in partnership programs for the purpose of securing, advancing, or changing careers.
> Ninety-one percent of those who obtained new positions after graduation were working in jobs related to their field of study.
> Forty-three percent of those who had jobs prior to graduating report receiving pay increases within six months of graduating and eighty-three percent of those attributed the increase to completing their degree.
> More than half (52%) of those who had jobs prior to graduating are enjoying greater responsibility, and two-thirds of them attribute this increase to the fact that they got their degree at the UP.
> Half of all University Partnership graduates who were promoted advanced into new positions following their graduation. Of those, 71% indicated their salaries were substantially increased.
> Ninety-one percent of UP grads in new jobs after graduation report having increased responsibility in those new positions.

Whether you refer to LCCC's University Partnership as "the bargain in your backyard" or "the best value in Ohio," one thing is certain: It allows for affordable access to parts of the higher education continuum that normally individuals would not consider. The LCCC University Partnership is one where all parties benefit.

References

Ballinger, Marcia. (2006). How community colleges and universities collaborate to enhance the college-going rate in Ohio [Monograph Number 1]. *Invitational Working Conference—Community Colleges: Partnerships with Ohio Universities.* David L. Meabon (Ed.). Toledo, OH: The John H. Russel Center for Educational Leadership, The University of Toledo.

Day, Jennifer C., & Newman, Eric C. (2002). *The big payoff: Educational attainment and synthetic estimates of work-life earnings* (Current Population Reports, P23-210). Washington, DC: U.S. Census Bureau. Retrieved from https://www.census.gov/prod/2002pubs/p23-210.pdf

Gonzalez, Jennifer. (2011, June 12). Go to community college, earn a bachelor's degree: Florida likes that combination. *The Chronicle of Higher Education.* Retrieved from http://chronicle.com/article/Floridas-Community-Colleges/127880/

Lewin, Tamar. (2009, May 2). Community colleges challenge hierarchy with 4-year degrees. *The New York Times*. Retrieved from http://www.nytimes.com/2009/05/03/education/03community.html

Meaney, Alison. (2011, March 2). Lorain County Community College moves forward on North Ridgeville education center. *The Sun News*. Retrieved from http://blog.cleveland.com/thesun/2011/03/lorain_county_community_colleg_20.html.

12

THE COMPREHENSIVE COLLEGE BACCALAUREATE

An Idea Whose Time Has Come!

Andrew K. Koch and John N. Gardner

We start this chapter by asking you to indulge our act of personifying the term *idea* in our title. You see, we feel that an idea can have life—and, as a result, an idea can shape the lived experience and the overall human condition of which that lived experience is a part. We also feel—quite vehemently, in fact—that the comprehensive college baccalaureate (CCB) is one such idea. Thus, using an ontological metaphor in which we represent the nonliving comprehensive college baccalaureate as a person is, in our view, quite justifiable, because the comprehensive college baccalaureate is alive.

Unlike the Bride of Frankenstein, which was "alive" and viewed with horror, the comprehensive college baccalaureate—for a number of reasons that we will explore in this chapter—is a "living thing" worth celebrating, cultivating, and promoting. It is, in essence, a pathway to education that can promote growth for people and the communities of which they are a part. It is a means to a richer and more fulfilling life. It is an idea whose time has come.

But before we share and support our views about why the comprehensive college baccalaureate is needed and an important part of the future of higher education in the United States, we feel compelled to tell you who we are and why we have at least some reason to want to comment on the comprehensive college baccalaureate this time in the history of the nation we call home.

The first author, Andrew K. Koch, has worked in higher education for nearly twenty years. He possesses a terminal degree in American studies, and, in addition to leading and writing about student success efforts in postsecondary education, he has conducted research on the role of colleges and universities in shaping culture and democracy in the United States. He currently is the executive vice president of the John N. Gardner Institute for Excellence in Undergraduate Education; a nonprofit higher-education center that works with colleges and universities to help them create strategic plans for student success and institutional excellence.

The second author, John N. Gardner, also possesses a graduate degree in American studies, and he is the founder and current leader of the aforementioned higher-education center. In fact, this is the second higher-education center that he has founded and led— the first being the National Resource Center for the First-Year Experience and Students in Transition at the University of South Carolina, where he was also a professor and administrator for over thirty years. A higher education change agent who has focused considerable energy on calling more attention to the importance of the first year of college and improving assessment of the entirety of the beginning college experience, Gardner's experiences as a faculty member, an administrator, and a speaker on postsecondary education practice and policy have allowed him to reflect on and shape higher education in the United States during the latter 20th and early 21st centuries. In fact, it was during one such reflection opportunity—while giving an address to what was then called the Community College Baccalaureate Association—that Gardner suggested that the group use the name "Comprehensive College Baccalaureate Association," because he felt it better reflected the unique mission for the institutions that made up the organization.

Together, we, the authors of this chapter, will use our academic preparation as American culture researchers, knowledge gleaned by working with hundreds of dynamic two-year and four-year higher-education institutions across the United States, and a variety of other administrative and academic experiences as sources for our perspective on why the CCB is an important vehicle for the improvement and future success of higher education in the United States. Specifically, we will use this chapter to address five factors that make the CCB necessary, including: demographics, public policy directions, issues associated with transferring from a two-year to a four-year institution, supply-and-demand issues associated with professional programs, and costs to students and states. By doing so, we feel that we will offer ample evidence to justify our claim that the comprehensive college baccalaureate is an idea whose time has come.

Raisons d'être—Factors That Give Life to the Comprehensive College Baccalaureate

Demographics

According to one of the United States Census Bureau's most recent census reports (2006), between 2000 and 2005, the growth rate for persons classified as racial minorities exceeded the national average rate of growth (5%) for all racial classifications. The Black population increased 6%, the American Indian and Alaska Native population increased 7%, the Pacific Islander population had a 12% gain, and the growth rate for people who classified themselves as "Two or More Races" was 17%. The largest growth among racial groups came from persons who classified themselves as Hispanic—this group increasing by 21%.

During the same decade, the proportion of Americans living below the poverty level increased dramatically. After analyzing data collected for the 2010 Census, the Census Bureau issued a report (2010) showing that "the number of people in poverty in 2010 (46.2 million) is the largest number in the 52 years for which poverty estimates have been published."

These data merit sharing because, when it comes to both enrolling and succeeding in college, race and class matter. It is beyond the scope of our chapter to summarize decades of scholarship on the effect of race and income on college attendance and completion rates. It suffices for us to write that this body of scholarship is quite large, and quite consistent in its findings. Persons from the aforementioned racial classifications and/or from low-income profiles—and the latter includes poverty-stricken White students as well as low-income students from racial minority classifications—are significantly less likely to attend college to begin with, and comparably less likely to complete their programs of study even if they do enroll in postsecondary education. Even when persons from these backgrounds do go to college, they are often the first in their families to do so—meaning that they lack the cultural capital possessed by students coming from families with parents and/or siblings with college degrees. This lack of contextual competency further decreases the likelihood of success in college in general which, in turn, further diminishes the likelihood that these students will complete a baccalaureate degree.

The comprehensive college baccalaureate movement offers a ray of hope in this otherwise depressing set of circumstances—and that ray of hope might just be what is needed for the United States to realize a brighter future. With their direct linkage to open access community colleges—the form of postsecondary institution that enrolls the greatest proportion of low-income, first-generation, and/or racial minority students in the United States (Bailey, Jenkins, & Leinbach, 2005)—comprehensive college baccalaureate programs serve precisely the same portion of the population that is least likely to go to and succeed in traditional forms of postsecondary education in the United States. Comprehensive baccalaureate programs can provide these students with a new, direct, viable option for obtaining a baccalaureate degree.

We explore the transferability of credit benefits associated with the direct connection that occurs when a community college is affiliated with comprehensive college baccalaureate degree programs later in this chapter. But alluding to those benefits here is merited—because the connection between a community college and comprehensive college baccalaureate degree programs can provide clear pathways for better education and the better life that comes with it for the population segments that are historically least likely to garner these educational benefits. As the data shared at the beginning of this section show, these are the same population segments experiencing the greatest growth in the United States during the latter 20th and early 21st centuries. In short, for reasons associated with demographics, the comprehensive college baccalaureate is an idea whose time has come.

Public Policy (and Public Pressure)

The demographic trends mentioned in the previous section have not gone unobserved by policy makers in the United States. Recognizing that a healthy economy requires a well-educated workforce, and realizing that workforce needs will not be met if current postsecondary student attrition rates are left unchecked, policy groups as varied as the National Governors Association, the federal Department of Education, and philanthropic organizations, such as Lumina Foundation for Education and the Bill and Melinda Gates Foundation, have all called for and advanced efforts to increase college participation, success, and completion. Whether one considers Lumina Foundation's "Goal 2025" initiative, the National Governors Association's "Compete to Complete" effort, or President Obama's 2020 completion goal, one point is clear: Completion is not just a nice idea; it is a shared national priority.

At the same time that an array of groups are advocating for greater postsecondary degree production, pressures associated with rankings and public perception seem to be acting as a countervailing force. Ironically, some of the very same governors calling for greater degree completion are, simultaneously, promoting strategies that would make their public flagship and public regional comprehensive institutions more selective—meaning they would be smaller and less accessible to many students. In August 2011, during a meeting with the Kansas Board of Regents, Kansas Governor Sam Brownback, pointing to his state's higher education institutions' respective positions in the *U.S. News and World Report* annual college edition, urged Kansas's colleges and universities to raise admission standards to boost each institution's standings in the national rankings (Carpenter, 2011). He is not the only governor to call for greater selectivity in their state's public four-year institution sector.

Governors such as Brownback may very well just be reflecting and reacting to the broader public's desires. As the journalist and novelist Tom Wolfe (2005) lamented in his foreword to the acclaimed *Declining by Degrees: Higher Education at Risk*, "Parents in large cities and many smaller ones" have been "succumbing in droves to the mad compulsion to cover their families with glory by getting their children into the very best colleges as rated each fall by *U.S. News and World Report*." If and when members of the public wonder who to fault for what Wolfe called "(t)he pandemic known as college mania," they might just need to look into the mirror for the answer.

The dynamic that leads to calls for greater numbers of college graduates from some of the same people who also advocate for decreased flow of students into higher education institutions reminds us of Dr. Dolittle's two-headed pushmi-pullyu. Like this gazelle-unicorn mix, which found both of its respective heads attempting to go in opposite directions whenever it tried to move, the nation's postsecondary education goals will get nowhere if these counteracting approaches are left to continue without an alternative. If more baccalaureate degrees are to be a part of the completion agenda being promoted by public policy makers—and many states as well as the federal government are advocating for them to be—then baccalaureate degrees must come from a source other than the existing four-year public postsecondary institutions that are being compelled by many to narrow their doorways in order to enhance their reputations. The comprehensive college baccalaureate can be that source.

With well-developed, direct relationships with open access two-year institutions—which, at least for now, operate at a safe distance from rankings and the public pressure associated therewith—comprehensive college baccalaureate programs can be a prime producer—if not *the* prime producer—for the increased numbers of baccalaureate degree holders called for by public policy makers. In short, when one considers the confusing conflict between higher education public policy goals (on one hand) and public pressure for high status in the established four-year public university sector (on the other), it becomes clear why the comprehensive college baccalaureate is an idea whose time has come.

The Need to Terminate Transfer Trauma

From their earliest origins as "junior colleges," community colleges were created to offer students the opportunity to conduct the first two years of study for an academic program that could ultimately lead to a baccalaureate degree. But to realize that baccalaureate degree goal, students must experience success during the transfer transition process—in other words, shifting from the two-year to the four-year institution "lane" should not be a cause for falling off the road to degree completion. Alas, far too many students fail to successfully make the transfer transition; and this lack of transfer success is a serious threat to the nation's degree completion goals.

For example, in a 2009 study, Bridget Terry Long and Michal Kurlaender compared the outcomes of community college students who transferred into public four-year institutions in Ohio to those of similar students who initially enrolled within the Ohio public four-year higher education sector—to see if starting in a community college was a benefit or hindrance to students. Even when controlling for a host of variables, including standardized test scores, students who initially began at community colleges were 14.5% less likely to complete bachelor's degrees within nine years when compared with their counterparts who started at four-year institutions. Sadly, this does not surprise us.

We believe that far too often, faculty and administrators at two-year and four-year institutions alike make erroneous assumptions about their transfer students. It is a popular myth that transfer students "know how to do college." Credit articulation agreements are not enough—because, although these articulation agreements may help fit together credits, they do little to help humans feel as if they fit. Rarely do the two-year institutions have programs targeted at their transfer-bound students to specifically address transfer transition preparation, and four-year institutions are equally unlikely to have well-developed programs or policies that address the needs of the transfer students that they receive. Despite the fact that the four-year environment will probably be vastly different than the two-year environment from which they are coming, four-year institutions rarely require transfer students to attend orientation. Four-year and two-year institutions alike rarely know the success rates of the transfer students that they respectively receive or send. In the limited instances where some transfer support programs do exist, rarely are they intentionally connected, assessed, and coordinated by some form of overarching transfer success plan.

The absence of these programs and plans results in stress and confusion for many transfer students—and all too often that stress and duress culminate in the abandonment of baccalaureate degree dreams and goals. Although it is easy and often the case for both the sending and receiving institutions to blame these transfer students for their lack of success, doing so is tantamount to blaming the victim in many instances. When transfer students put forth adequate effort, they should not be punished because of lack of a coherent set of processes, programs, and policies at their sending or receiving institutions. Unfortunately, our experience and data, such as that which we shared in this section, show that this is far too often the case. The transfer transition is unnecessarily traumatic, and this trauma is a significant factor in the lackluster baccalaureate degree completion rates for community college students who transfer to four-year institutions.

We do not think that two-year and four-year institutions should leave addressing these transfer trauma issues to "someone else." In fact, this is why we work with two-year institutions to create strategic plans for success for their transfer-bound students and with four-year institutions to create strategic plans for their transfer-receiving functions. But one way to make sure that the trauma associated with transferring to earn a baccalaureate is eliminated is to eliminate that transfer process all together. This is where comprehensive college baccalaureate programs come into play.

Offered by the same institutions that provide the first two years of instruction, comprehensive college baccalaureate programs nullify the aforementioned issues associated with transfer, because they make it possible for students to not have to transfer at all. They put to rest any issues associated with transferability of credit, because the courses originate from the same educational organization that is offering the baccalaureate degree. They negate institutional cultural and context competency issues common to transfer students in new institutional environments, because, without transfer, the institutional context and culture remains the same for the students involved in the comprehensive college baccalaureate degree programs. In summation, because they eliminate issues associated with transfer trauma, the comprehensive college baccalaureate is an idea whose time has come.

Supply and Demand for Space in Professional Programs

At the same time that comprehensive college baccalaureate programs are eliminating transfer trauma issues, they are simultaneously addressing public demand for academic programs associated with professions such as health care and education—fields that flagship public research universities and many regional comprehensive four-year institutions tend to underserve. Before we continue with this line of thought, we want to acknowledge that we have high regard for research universities—we have worked in and earned degrees from institutions of this genre and feel that their mission is important to the well-being of the states and nation of which they are a part. But we have observed that four-year institutions that place a heavy or even partial emphasis on research tend to expend their resources and energy in a manner that neglects practical programs of studies. This may be a by-product of the culture of research institutions—where theory has historically had higher status than practice. We also must observe that, amidst this historical and cultural context, the "practical programs" that do have a strong foothold in research institutions tend to be those in historically male-dominated fields, such as engineering, science, and business.

It is within this context that comprehensive college baccalaureate degree programs can flourish. Take, for example, nursing programs. The population in the United States is steadily expanding. This expansion is the result of both a combination of growth in numbers of citizens in general and increases in average life span owing to advances in medicine. As a result, the nation's population is expected to grow by 13% over the next decade and a half. The field of nursing should be growing to meet the demands associated with this expanding population. Yet the four-year higher-education sector is not keeping pace with these needs.

According to a policy brief issued by the American Association of State Colleges and Universities (AASCU), "by 2020, experts believe there will be a national shortage of registered nurses reaching more than 800,000." The AASCU report (2005) continues, "According to the U.S. Department of Health and Human Services, 44 states and the District of Columbia are expected to have nursing shortages by 2020 impacting hospitals, nursing homes, ambulatory care and schools."

Four-year colleges and universities have attempted to expand their nursing programs, but their efforts have not adequately addressed the issue. Citing resource limitations, space in four-year nursing programs remains limited, and many qualified applicants are turned away. According to AASCU (2005), more than 36,000 qualified applicants were rejected from baccalaureate degree-granting nursing programs in 2003–2004. This trend does not bode well for efforts to abate the pending nursing shortage.

With their established two-year nursing programs serving as a teaching and learning foundation, and a firm focus on teaching as opposed to costly research, comprehensive college baccalaureate nursing programs are well positioned to use their resources to address the gap between the number of nurses that current four-year programs produce and the number of nurses that will be needed by the U.S. population of 2020. This kind of workforce-related supply and demand meeting function is not merely limited to nursing. In *The Community College Baccalaureate: Emerging Trends and Policy Issues*, Deborah Floyd, Michael Skolnik, and Kenneth Walker (2005) describe how comprehensive college baccalaureate programs are meeting local workforce needs throughout the nation. For example, in addition to addressing needs in the nursing field, the CCB programs at St. Petersburg College are also addressing degree production shortfalls in applied fields, such as teacher education, technology management, dental hygiene, orthodontics, and prosthetics. Comparably, three community colleges in Hawaii are authorized to provide baccalaureate degrees in the fields of business and information technology, computer electronic technology, and culinary arts.

In summation, comprehensive college baccalaureate degree programs address public demand for education in fields that four-year institutions are not adequately addressing. As evidenced by the examples provided, these fields are literally vital to the health of the nation. This form of education also has implications for the economic well-being of the persons who earn the degrees as well as the employers they serve and the communities in which they reside. These are yet additional reasons why we can confidently assert that the comprehensive college baccalaureate is an idea whose time has come!

Costs to Students and States

According to the aforementioned AASCU policy brief (2005), one of the main reasons cited by four-year institutions for their inability to expand nursing programs was the cost associated with the human resources and related overhead necessary to teach and support additional students and do research in the field. Adding highly trained faculty in nursing programs at four-year institutions where research is a hallmark is simply cost prohibitive. The Great Recession has created many uncertainties; but amidst this uncertainty, one thing is clear—in an era of diminished resources, cost factors that prevent growth in nursing at four-year institutions are not merely applicable to that field.

According to research conducted by the State Higher Education Executive Officers ([SHEEO], 2010), over the past decade, educational appropriations per full-time student reached a high in FY 2001, followed by four years of decline during the period spanning FY 2002 to FY 2005 as a result of the 2001 recession. Per-student funding increased again in the three fiscal years that fell between 2006 and 2008. However, in FY 2009, the bottom fell out. Sparked by the recession, appropriations per student fell as states struggled with massive revenue shortfalls. In fact, in 2009 appropriations per student remained lower (in constant dollars) than in most years since FY 1980. And FY 2010, 2011, and 2012 funding levels have proven to be even worse.

In an environment where cash-strapped state budgets have led to less funding for public four-year institutions, and during an era in which more students find themselves with considerably diminished financial capacity owing to unemployment or other germane hardships, the difference between missing and realizing the baccalaureate degree–related targets associated with the nation's college completion agenda lies, in part, with the nation's ability to provide low-cost, high-quality baccalaureate degree program options.

Comprehensive college baccalaureate degree programs offer students the opportunity to both start and finish baccalaureate degrees in a low-cost environment—the community colleges with which these degree programs are affiliated. By offering students clear pathways for blending community college and university course work all in the same institutional environment, and doing so in a manner that allows students to continue living at home and commuting short distances—perhaps even while continuing in the jobs they held while working on their associate degrees—the comprehensive college baccalaureate can reduce cost to students and, by extension, to the institutions and state taxpayers who help to support their education. This can allow limited public funding streams to be stretched further—thereby offering more students the opportunity to obtain a baccalaureate degree even with a diminished public funding resource pool. Thus, the potential to yield more baccalaureate degrees in environments that bear lower costs to both students and state treasuries are yet another reason why the comprehensive college baccalaureate is an idea whose time has come.

Summary and Conclusions—Life, Liberty, and the Pursuit of Happiness

Despite the fact that we have made connections between baccalaureate degree attainment and workforce and economic benefits, to us, education is about something more than a pathway to a paycheck and the fabrication of a skilled labor force on which corporations can draw. Although we have made clear connections between five factors that give great credence to the existence and expansion of comprehensive college baccalaureate degree programs—(1) demographics, (2) public policy directions, (3) issues associated with transferring from a two-year to a four-year institution, (4) supply-and-demand issues associated with professional programs, and, (5) costs to students and states—in our view, these factors take a backseat to the reason why higher education matters to begin with. To a greater or lesser extent, these factors all are market-based. Although we consider ourselves capitalists, we are social capitalists—that is, we do not believe that the market is perfect; nor do we believe in the accumulation of capital for the sake of accumulation. There needs to be some socially redeeming value in education—and that value must advance social justice. Gordon Gekko should not be setting higher-education policy at the national, state, and institutional levels.

During a period when some have questioned the public benefit of higher education, we assert that one of the greatest benefits that the comprehensive college baccalaureate can provide the public of the United States is an educated citizenry. Like Thomas Jefferson, we believe that an educated citizenry is a vital requisite for our survival as a free people. Given the demographic that they serve and the necessities of our democracy, the comprehensive college baccalaureate offers social mobility and the enfranchisement associated therewith. It is a pathway to life, liberty, and the pursuit of happiness. And for this reason—in conjunction with yet above all other reasons—the comprehensive college baccalaureate is an idea whose time has come!

References

American Association of State Colleges and Universities. (2005). Higher education's role in solving the national nursing shortage. *AASCU Policy Matters.* Retrieved from http://www.aascu.org/uploadedFiles/AASCU/Content/Root/PolicyAndAd vocacy/PolicyPublications/Nursing%20Shortage.pdf

Bailey, T., Jenkins, D., & Leinbach, T. (2005, January). *What we know about community college low-income and minority student outcomes: Descriptive statistics from national surveys*. New York, NY: Community College Research Center Teachers College. Retrieved from http://www.eric.ed.gov/PDFS/ED484354.pdf

Carpenter, T. (2011, August 17). Brownback seeks higher academic rankings. *Topeka Capital-Journal*. Retrieved from http://cjonline.com/news/2011-08-17/brown back-seeks-higher-academic-rankings

Floyd, D. L., Skolnik, M. L., & Walker, K. B. (2005). *The community college baccalaureate: Emerging trends and policy issues*. Sterling, VA: Stylus.

Hersh, R. H., & Merrow, J. (2005). *Declining by degrees: Higher education at risk*. New York, NY: Palgrave MacMillan.

Long, B. T., & Kurlaender, M. (2009, March). Do community colleges provide a viable pathway to a baccalaureate degree? *Educational Evaluation and Policy Analysis, 31*(1). 30–53.

State Higher Education Executive Officers. (2010). *State higher education finance FY 2009*. Boulder, CO: SHEEO.

U.S. Census Bureau. (2006). *Race and Hispanic origin in 2005*. Washington, DC: U.S. Census Bureau. Retrieved from www.census.gov/population/pop-profile/ dynamic/RACEHO.pdf

U.S. Census Bureau. (2010). *Income, poverty and health insurance in the United States: 2010—Highlights*. Washington, DC: U.S. Census Bureau. Retrieved from http://www.census.gov/hhes/www/poverty/data/incpovhlth/2010/highlights.html

Wolfe, T. (2005). Foreword. In R. H. Hersh & J. Merrow (Eds.), *Declining by degrees: Higher education at risk* (pp. ix–xi). New York, NY: Palgrave MacMillan.

Marcia J. Ballinger was appointed to serve in the role of provost and vice president for academic and learner services in July 2011. She has served in several leadership positions at Lorain County Community College for the past 20 years. Prior to assuming the provost's role, she was vice president for strategic and institutional development for 9 years and vice president of the LCCC Foundation. In that role, she led LCCC's institutional advancement efforts that focused on the major development initiatives set forth in LCCC's vision. Her direct experience with the University Partnership included serving on the initial steering committee and team that created the concept for the partnership. Additionally, she spearheaded the community levy campaign that created the foundational funding for the University Partnership in 1995. Subsequently, she provided the strategy for the increased funding for the University Partnership in 2004 and is currently in the initial planning phase for the 2013 ballot. She holds an MBA from Kent State University, which she completed as a University Partnership student, and is now completing her PhD in higher education from Walden University. She serves on numerous boards, including the Workforce Investment Board, Children's Services, Workforce Institute, among others. She currently cochairs two major LCCC initiatives focused on student success and completion, which are Completion by Design and Achieving the Dream.

Tom Benberg is an experienced educator, having served in various educational positions for nearly 50 years. He began his career in elementary and secondary education as a teacher, principal and superintendent. Thereafter, he served institutions of higher education as a faculty member, executive vice president, and acting president. His present position is that of vice president and chief of staff for the Southern Association of Colleges and Schools Commission on Colleges.

Tom has been with the Commission for 15 years and has been active in consulting with institutions, helping to train peer review committees, and in serving the advisory needs of The Board of Trustees.

Tom holds an EdD degree in curriculum and instruction from Texas A&M University–Commerce, a master's degree from Indiana University, and a baccalaureate degree from Ouachita Baptist University.

Debra D. Bragg's research focuses on transition to college by youth and adults, especially student populations that have not attended college historically. She is particularly interested in how underserved youth and adult students (minority, low income, first-generation, immigrant students) use the community college to transition to higher education, including how public policies position community colleges as a primary port of entry. The expanding mission of community colleges, including the increasing importance of linkages to high schools, adult education, postsecondary education and the workforce is of particular interest. She is the director of the Office of Community College Research and Leadership (OCCRL), a research organization that she founded at the University of Illinois in 1989.

Chris Bustamante, EdD, serves as president of Rio Salado College, the largest in head count of the ten Maricopa Community Colleges located in metropolitan Phoenix, and the largest online community college in the nation. Rio Salado serves approximately 58,000 credit and an additional 11,000 noncredit students annually, of which 43,000 are online students.

Dr. Bustamante was appointed to this position in June 2010 after serving as the college's interim president, vice president of community development and student services, and dean of academic affairs. Earlier in his career, he served in senior level government affairs positions for the Maricopa Community College District. He is well known as an advocate for increasing access to higher education opportunities. He has forged transformational partnerships with business, government, and other educational providers, leading to innovations such as the first Communiversity to be established west of the Mississippi River. Dr. Bustamante currently serves as an adjunct professor for Northern Arizona University in the Master's of Educational Leadership Program.

Before joining the Maricopa Community Colleges District, Dr. Bustamante served as the assistant to the superintendent for Community and Government Relations for the Phoenix Union High School District. Dr. Bustamante also served as a legislative aide to the Arizona House of Representatives from 1984 to 1987.

Dr. Marie Cini has spent her career as a faculty member and administrator working with adult students. She earned her PhD in social psychology from the University of Pittsburgh in 1994. She has published and presented on leadership development online, the structure of distance learning units in colleges and universities, and organizational culture and distance education.

Dr. John R. Crooks is the associate provost of the University Partnership at Lorain County Community College. He has also served as the dean of science and mathematics and the director of distance learning at LCCC. Prior to arriving at LCCC, Dr. Crooks was chair of the Division of Science, Mathematics and Computer Science and associate professor of biology at Iowa Wesleyan College. Dr. Crooks received his BS and MS in biology from Northeast Missouri State University (now Truman State University) and his PhD in biology from Bowling Green State University. He is a life member of the Missouri Academy of Science, the Ohio Academy of Science, and Sigma Xi, The Scientific Research Society. He also has memberships in American Association for the Advancement of Science, the Community College Baccalaureate Association, and serves as the college's liaison for the Council for Undergraduate Research. Dr. Crooks has received grants from the National Science Foundation, the Ohio Department of Education, and the Ohio Board of Regents. He is a member of the following boards: The Ohio Academy of Science, The Ohio Mathematics and Science Coalition, and REACHigher (Lorain County's P-16 Council). Dr. Crooks has served on the Ohio K–12 Academic Content Standards Science Writing Team and developed a Young Women in STEM summer camp for middle school girls. He is a reviewer for the Albert Einstein Distinguished Educator Fellowship Program, Higher Learning Commission (AQIP), *Journal of College Student Retention*, Science Books & Films, and Science Netlinks.

Dr Carol D'Amico served as the executive vice president of Ivy Tech Community College of Indiana and was responsible for the development Ivy Tech's statewide strategy and programming in workforce development as a boost to the state's economy. She is a recognized expert on education and workforce development issues, coauthor of the nationally recognized *Workforce 2020,* and frequent lecturer and keynoter with extensive experience in advising corporate and government leaders on strategies to strengthen America's economy through a qualified educated workforce.

Appointed by President Bush in 2001, Dr. D'Amico served as the assistant secretary for the Office of Vocational and Adult Education until 2003. She was the principal spokesperson and leading advisor to the president and secretary of Education on all matters related to high school reform, community/technical colleges, and adult literacy.

D'Amico holds an EdD in higher education leadership and policy studies and a master's degree in adult education and organizational development from Indiana University.

Dr. Angela M. Garcia Falconetti is the vice president for institutional advancement at Virginia Western Community College. Prior to serving Virginia Western, Angela was vice president for planning, development, and institutional effectiveness at Daytona State College. Angela also served as interim vice president for institutional advancement and executive director of the Daytona State College Foundation.

Prior to joining Daytona State, Angela completed an endowed postdoctoral fellowship with The University of Texas at Austin's Community College Leadership Program and the U.S. Department of Education in Washington, DC. As postdoctoral fellow, Angela worked as research associate for the Community College Survey of Student Engagement and the Survey of Entering Student Engagement. Angela also served as special assistant for the first deputy assistant secretary for community colleges, Office of Vocational and Adult Education.

Angela serves as editorial board member for the *Community College Journal of Research and Practice* and served as associate editor for *The Journal of College Orientation and Transition*. Angela received the 2007 national research award from the National Orientation Directors Association, the 2007 University of North Florida's Outstanding Dissertation Award, and the 2003 University of North Florida's Outstanding Academic Advisor Award. Formerly, Angela was an assistant vice president for student affairs at the University of North Florida.

Professor Deborah L. Floyd joined Florida Atlantic University in 2001 after 26 years of service in higher education in Texas, Iowa, Virginia, and Kentucky. Her administrative career has included service as a dean and vice president of student affairs, a community college president and a special assistant to a university chancellor. She also served as a senior fellow with the Association of American Colleges and Universities, the Board of Directors of the American Association of Community Colleges, secretary of the American

College Personnel Association, and is a past president of the Council for the Study of Community Colleges. In 2011, she was named as editor in chief of the 35-year-old peer reviewed journal, *The Community College Journal of Research and Practice.*

Dr. John N. Gardner is a professor and higher education change agent whose principal interest is calling more attention to the importance of the first year of college for new and transfer students and improving assessment of the entirety of the beginning college experience. Toward this end, he has led a 30-year international reform movement to persuade colleges to change their approaches to working with their first-year students. He is the founder of two national centers, The National Resource Center for the First-Year Experience and Students in Transition at the University of South Carolina, and the John N. Gardner Institute for Excellence in Undergraduate Education (formerly the Policy Center on the First Year of College) based in Brevard, North Carolina. His first college teaching experiences were at a rural, open admissions two-year college in South Carolina. Later in his career, he served as vice chancellor for academic affairs for five such two-year colleges in South Carolina.

Dr. Andrew K. Koch is a staunch advocate for higher education in general and an agent of change and improvement in undergraduate education in particular. Currently serving as executive vice president of the John N. Gardner Institute for Excellence in Undergraduate Education, Dr. Koch has worked for two decades in postsecondary education. During that time, he garnered substantive practical experience with undergraduate education administration, strategic planning, fund-raising, enrollment management, institutional and public education policy efforts, and a host of other endeavors designed to enhance student access to and success in college. Dr. Koch is also the author of numerous publications focused on higher education improvement and student success.

Edith Pendleton serves as the dean of learning resources at Edison State College. Pendleton's research focuses on the community college baccalaureate movement and its impact on underserved and minority students historically disenfranchised from upward mobility due to an inability to succeed within the university system. She brings 12 years of experience as a science journalist, including assignments with *Science News* magazine, *National Geographic* magazine, and the Appalachian Regional Commission in Washington, DC. Pendleton received a bachelor's and master's degree in journalism from the University of Missouri and a doctorate from the University of South Florida.

Nancy Remington holds a PhD from the University of Nevada in educational leadership. Her 30-year teaching experience in Nevada spans the spectrum of preschool through graduate school. As an English and education faculty member at Great Basin College, she developed and implemented the first baccalaureate degree program in teacher education. Particularly passionate about effective professional development for teachers and administrators, she was the founding director of the Great Basin Writing Project and the Nevada Regional Professional Development Program. She has worked as an evaluator for the Northeastern Nevada Regional Professional Development Program, and currently, she serves on the Board of the Nevada Women's Fund, as an editor for the Community College Baccalaureate Association online journal *The Journal of the New Comprehensive College* as well as working as an educational consultant and as a field director with the National Writing Project.

Ronald Remington holds a PhD from the University of Nevada in cognitive psychology. With 35 years' experience as a faculty member and administrator in higher education in three states, he has served as a commissioner for Northwest Commission on Colleges and Universities and as president of two Nevada community colleges. During his tenure at Great Basin College and the Community College of Southern Nevada, he pioneered innovative baccalaureate degrees in education, applied sciences, professional studies, and dental hygiene. He currently works as an educational consultant and serves on the Board of Directors for the Community College Baccalaureate Association.

John Patrick Rice is the chief development officer at Great Basin College (GBC)–Elko, Nevada. Prior to joining the college's administration, Rice was a member of the faculty where he was on the team that developed the first bachelor degree program at GBC. He subsequently chaired the college's faculty senate and helped to develop and shepherd two additional bachelor degree programs through the Nevada System of Higher Education Board of Regents for approval. His nearly 20 years of experience in higher education has been spent entirely in the rural, comprehensive college setting. He has been invited to speak on community college and economic and workforce development issues in a variety of venues, including the United States Senate

Rural Steering Committee and the White House Summit on Community Colleges. He earned his MFA from the University of Wisconsin–Milwaukee and his PhD from Capella University. He and his wife, Loretta, have a daughter, Olivia.

Lisa Romano-Arnold has spent her career as an advocate for community college transfer students and has been instrumental in creating a partnership model for seamless transfer to create student access for baccalaureate attainment while emphasizing associate degree completion. In her position, Lisa oversees 25 advisors and outreach specialists who provide transfer transitional support services to more than 80 community colleges across the country, including all 16 Maryland community colleges.

She began her career at the College of Southern Maryland (formerly Charles County Community College) as an administrator and faculty member and moved to University of Maryland University College (UMUC) in 2003 to assume the position of associate director. Lisa is currently a doctoral student at UMUC enrolled in the doctor of management in community college policy and administration program.

Dr. Alene Bycer Russell has served as senior state policy consultant to the American Association of State Colleges and Universities (AASCU) in Washington, DC, since 2004. In this capacity, she tracks, analyzes, and communicates state policy trends on key higher education topics, including college access and student success, teacher preparation, and data systems and accountability. Dr. Russell has also worked for several years as a consultant to the National Center for Education Statistics, U.S. Department of Education. Prior to this, she was a senior research associate at the State Higher Education Executive Officers (SHEEO) association in Denver, Colorado, working there for 11 years. Before joining SHEEO, she worked as institutional research coordinator at Loretto Heights College in Denver.

Dr. Russell received a PhD in sociology from the University of Chicago, with training in survey research at the National Opinion Research Center. She holds bachelor's and master's degrees in sociology from the University of Pennsylvania.

Collin M. Ruud is a visiting project coordinator at the University of Illinois' Office of Community College Research and Leadership. Mr. Ruud is also a PhD candidate at the University of Illinois, studying higher education. He received his master's of education in higher education at the University of

Illinois and has also studied at the University of Missouri–Kansas City. At OCCRL, Mr. Ruud studies applied baccalaureate degrees for a project sponsored by the National Science Foundation, midpoint credentials for Lumina Foundation for Education, and other policies that affect college degree attainment. Collin's research interests include college student development, student affairs, high school to postsecondary transitions, and technology in higher education. He previously has worked as a research assistant in the Office of the Vice President for Technology and Economic Development and has worked for two years as an administrator in residence halls.

Michael L. Skolnik is a professor emeritus in the University of Toronto where he previously held the William G. Davis Chair in Community College Leadership and directed the PhD program in Community College Leadership. Michael has conducted research on higher education for more than 40 years, and he has published extensively on many topics in higher education, including the organization and governance of postsecondary education, quality assurance, and the relationship between community colleges and universities. He was the first recipient of the Higher Education Research Award of the Canadian Society for the Study of Higher Education, and he received the Edward F. Sheffield Award for the best article of the year 2010 in the *Canadian Journal of Higher Education.* He has also served on the board of the quality assessment agency in Ontario that developed the quality standards for baccalaureate programs in Ontario community colleges and reviews proposals from the colleges to offer baccalaureate programs.

Dr. Linda M. Thor is chancellor of the Foothill-De Anza Community College District, serving the Silicon Valley of California. A nationally recognized innovator in education, before joining FHDA in February 2010, Dr. Thor served for nearly 20 years as president of Rio Salado College in Tempe, Arizona, a college known for serving working adults through online learning and worksite training. Prior to becoming Rio Salado's president in 1990, Dr. Thor was president of West Los Angeles College in Culver City, California. Dr. Thor's appointment as WLAC president in March 1986 followed a successful tenure as senior director of occupational and technical education and director of communications services for the Los Angeles Community College District.

Active at the national level, she serves on the boards of the League for Innovation in the Community College, the executive council of the WICHE Cooperative for Educational Technologies, the Commission on Lifelong

Learning for the American Council of Education, and the board of the Community College Baccalaureate Association. In 2010 she was appointed by U.S. Secretary of Education Arne Duncan to the Committee on Measures of Student Success.

Dr. Thor holds a bachelor's degree in journalism from Pepperdine University, a master's of public administration degree from California State University–Los Angeles and a doctor of education degree in community college administration from Pepperdine University.

Dr. Kenneth P. Walker served as the district president of Edison State College in Ft. Myers, Florida, for 20 years. He previously held college presidencies and other administrative positions in Oklahoma and Texas. He has a BA and an MA in political science, a PhD in higher education administration from the University of Texas–Austin, and continuing education in management and leadership from Harvard University, Southern Methodist University, College of William and Mary, and Oxford University. He served in the United States Air Force.

Dr. Walker has received numerous awards for exemplary and distinguished service, outstanding leadership in improving educational opportunities, and the advancement and support of education. He received the Professional Educators Award from the Association of Community College Trustees in 1977. He was honored in 2001 by the Edison State College District Board of Trustees with a unanimous Resolution naming the new $14 million Kenneth P. Walker Health Science Hall. Dr. Walker is now retired after more than 50 years of exemplary service to community colleges.

Dr. Belle S. Wheelan currently serves as president of the Southern Association of Colleges and Schools Commission on Colleges and is the first African American and the first woman to serve in this capacity. Her career spans more than 30 years and includes the roles of faculty member, chief student services officer, campus provost, college president, and secretary of Education. In several of those roles she was the first African American and/or woman to serve in those capacities.

Dr. Wheelan received her bachelor's degree from Trinity University in Texas (1972) with a double major in psychology and sociology, her master's from Louisiana State University (1974) in developmental educational psychology, and her doctorate from the University of Texas–Austin (1984) in educational administration with a special concentration in community college leadership.

She has received numerous awards and recognition, including four honorary degrees; the Distinguished Graduate Award from Trinity University (2002) and from the College of Education at the University of Texas–Austin (1992); *Washingtonian Magazine*'s 100 Most Powerful Women in Washington, DC (2001); the AAUW Woman of Distinction Award (2002); the Suanne Davis Roueche National Institute for Staff and Organizational Development's Distinguished Lecturer Award (2007); and the John E. Roueche National Institute for Staff and Organizational Development's International Leadership Award (2010).

She holds and has held membership in numerous local, state, and national organizations, including Rotary International; Alpha Kappa Alpha Sorority, Inc.; the American College Testing, Inc., board of directors; American Association of Community Colleges' board of directors; the Lumina Foundation for Education, board of directors; and the President's Round Table of the National Council on Black American Affairs.

Dr. Wheelan attributes her success to hard work, endurance, tenacity, and being in the right place at the right time. She recognizes that prayer and support from family and friends make anything possible.

INDEX

Topics include
- Strategies used at one two-year college that raised $50 million over ten years
- 101 boxed tips on the details that matter most
- Guidance for creating an institutional commitment to advancement
- Advice on how to enhance the advancement function
- Advice on how to build an effective foundation board that gives
- Advice on how to grow the Annual Fund with sustainable, repeatable gifts
- Approaches top universities use to close major gifts
- Guidance for using continuous quality improvement techniques to improve results year after year

Gateway to Opportunity
A History of the Community College in the United States
J. M. Beach
Foreword by W. Norton Grubb

"Beach's focus on the community college as an evolving social institution offers a perspective not found in earlier literature. . . . For readers interested in the history of the community college as a social institution, this book offers a concise treatment of its subject with numerous references to many important articles and texts that have reported on change and practice at the community college. Approaching the community college as a social institution offers a perspective that should be used more often to better understand the development, changes, and dilemmas in the history of this uniquely American experiment in post-secondary education." —*Community College Review*

22883 Quicksilver Drive
Sterling, VA 20166-2102

Subscribe to our e-mail alerts: www.Styluspub.com

Also available from Stylus

The Community College Baccalaureate
Emerging Trends and Policy Issues
Edited by Deborah L. Floyd, Michael L. Skolnik, and Kenneth P. Walker

"An important point to make early in this review is that the editors have taken care to present both supporting and opposing views to this trend. This comprehensive perspective is one of the strengths of this work, as all individuals concerned with the community college baccalaureate can use the book to consider both sides of the issue. In fact, one entire chapter is dedicated to presenting both positive and negative perspectives regarding the community college baccalaureate. A second strength of the book is that each chapter ends with a section of questions or issues for research and policy. One of the final chapters of the book then elaborates on common themes concerning research and policy that emerge in each of these sections. . . . This book is clearly valuable to policy makers, state legislators, faculty in community college or higher education programs and their students, and the community college constituencies of trustees, administrators, and faculty. . . . This book . . . will contribute greatly towards future research and policy decisions regarding the mission and role of the community college."—*Community College Journal of Research and Practice*

Community College Leadership
A Multidimensional Model for Leading Change
Pamela L. Eddy
Foreword by George R. Boggs

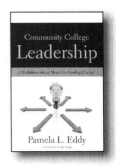

"Pamela L. Eddy's [book] deserves our time for two simple reasons: first, the multidimensional model for leading change transcends community colleges and is applicable broadly within and beyond education; and, second, the author's thoughtful inclusion of vignettes and case studies provides the day-to-day grounding to make her model relevant to readers of all professions. Yes, community college readers have the advantage of knowing many of the leadership challenges firsthand and will be more interested than most in sections such as 'Challenges of Community College Leadership,' but this book adds sufficiently to leadership literature that it should find itself on the bookshelves of professionals across education and the private sector." —*The Department Chair*

Fundraising Strategies for Community Colleges
The Definitive Guide for Advancement
Steve Klingaman

"Steve Klingaman's results-oriented strategies will benefit anyone ready to take a fresh look at their community college's fundraising. He provides a systematic approach to assessing what's effective, tackles barriers and myths, and offers countless practical, doable strategies that will instill confidence and produce positive results." —*Paul Heaton, Director of the Center for Community College Advancement, The Council for Advancement and Support of Education (CASE)*